Planning, Instruction, and Assessment

Effective Teaching Practices

Leslie W. Grant
Jennifer L. Hindman
James H. Stronge

Routledge
Taylor & Francis Group
New York London

First published 2010 by Eye On Education

Published 2013 by Routledge
711 Third Avenue, New York, NY 10017, USA
2 Park Square, Milton Park, Abingdon, Oxon OX14 4RN

Routledge is an imprint of the Taylor & Francis Group, an informa business

Library of Congress Cataloging-in-Publication Data

Grant, Leslie W., 1968-
  Planning, instruction, and assessment : effective teaching practices / Leslie W. Grant, Jennifer L. Hindman, James H. Stronge.
    p. cm.
  ISBN 978-1-59667-141-6
  1. Effective teaching. 2. Educational technology—Study and teaching. 3. Teaching—Training of. 4. Teachers—In-service training. I. Hindman, Jennifer L., 1971- II. Stronge, James H. III. Title.
  LB1025.3.G725 2010
  371.102—dc22
                                                                          2009042981

ISBN: 978-1-596-67141-6 (pbk)

Also Available from EYE ON EDUCATION

The James H. Stronge Research-to-Practice Series

**Planning, Instruction, and Assessment:
Effective Teaching Practices**
Leslie W. Grant, Jennifer L. Hindman, and James H. Stronge

**The Supportive Learning Environment:
Effective Teaching Practices**
Jennifer L. Hindman, Leslie W. Grant, and James H. Stronge

**Student Achievement Goal Setting: Using Data
to Improve Teaching and Learning**
James H. Stronge and Leslie W. Grant

Also available from these authors

**Handbook on Teacher Evaluation: Assessing
and Improving Performance**
James H. Stronge and Pamela D. Tucker

**Handbook on Educational Specialist Evaluation:
Assessing and Improving Performance**
James H. Stronge and Pamela D. Tucker

**Handbook on Teacher Portfolios for Evaluation
and Professional Development**
Pamela Tucker, James Stronge, and Christopher Gareis

Other great titles from Eye On Education

**Leading School Change: 9 Strategies to
Bring *Everybody* On Board**
Todd Whitaker

Classroom Walkthroughs to Improve Teaching and Learning
Donald S. Kachur, Judith A. Stout, and Claudia L. Edwards

Help Teachers Engage Students: Action Tools for Administrators
Annette Brinkman, Gary Forlini, and Ellen Williams

Dedication

This book is dedicated to the teachers who positively impacted our lives:

To my mother, my first teacher

LWG

To Dr. Robinson, my Summer Ventures field biology teacher

JLH

To my grandson Kaz

JHS

Acknowledgements

This book and its companion book, *The Supportive Learning Environment: Effective Teaching Practices* (Eye on Education, 2010) are the result of many workshops, studies, articles, and conversations with many individuals. Throughout the years, we have met many teachers, researchers, and administrators. Our interactions with them helped us to connect research to practice and we were inspired by the magic of their professional work from practice to research. Thank you to each of you, too numerous to acknowledge by name, who have impacted on our work.

The nexus of much of this work is coauthor James Stronge. He is like a Roman arch. His work facilitates the transportation of ideas much like the arches built centuries ago facilitated carrying water into the cities. Those who are privileged to interact with him can walk through the arch or benefit from the support of the arch. Over the years, James has involved us in effective teacher research and writing. As such our research interests in assessment, evaluation, and teacher selection have benefited from the collaboration.

We gratefully acknowledge the subscribers to the *Teacher Quality Digest* (a publication we self-published for three years) who supported our work to delve deeply into topics related to effective teachers. Their confidence in us inspired us, pushed us, and motivated us to identify relevant research and topics that represented a mix of the expected and the unexpected.

We would like to thank Mary Vause, a freelance copy editor and former graduate student in The College of William and Mary's School of Education. Mary completed her Master's in Education and is now a teacher. We benefited from editorial suggestions offered before the book was ever submitted to Eye On Education.

Also, we would like to acknowledge our colleague from Poquoson City Schools, Patricia J. McMahon, Ph.D., as a contributing author for her work on the Response-to-Intervention section found in Chapter 2.

Finally, we deeply appreciate Bob Sickles' commitment to recognizing the potential that a book has to contribute to the profession and his support in bringing a book from author's conception to publisher's birth.

About the Authors

Leslie W. Grant serves as a Visiting Assistant Professor in the School of Education at The College of William and Mary where she teaches in the teacher preparation and leadership preparation programs. Leslie is the coauthor of *Student Achievement Goal Setting: Using Data to Improve Teaching and Learning* (Eye On Education, 2009), *Teacher-made Assessments: How to Connect Curriculum, Instruction and Student Learning* (Eye on Education, 2008), and she is the contributing author to *Qualities of Effective Teachers* (2nd ed., 2007) authored by James H. Stronge and published by the Association for Supervision and Curriculum Development. Leslie provides consulting services in the area of classroom assessment and effective teaching.

Leslie has been a teacher, an instructional leader, and a content editor/item writer for a major test publishing company. She earned her doctoral degree in educational policy, planning and leadership from The College of William and Mary. She can be reached at grant_leslie@cox.net.

Jennifer L. Hindman is an education consultant and writer. Her passion is making learning relevant as she connects the tacit knowledge with the research base. She is the coauthor of *People First: The School Leader's Guide to Building and Cultivating Relationships with Teachers* (Eye on Education, 2009), *The Teacher Quality Index: A Protocol for Teacher Selection* (ASCD, 2006), and *Handbook for Qualities of Effective Teachers* (ASCD, 2004). She has been published in numerous state and national journals, including the *Journal of Personnel Evaluation in Education, Principal Leadership,* and *Educational Leadership.* She is the former editor of *The Teacher Quality Digest.* She consults in the areas of teacher selection and effective teaching.

Jennifer has been a teacher and science specialist. She earned her doctorate in educational policy, planning, and leadership from The College of William and Mary. She can be reached at jhindman@teacherqualityresources.com.

James H. Stronge is Heritage Professor in the Educational Policy, Planning, and Leadership Area at The College of William and Mary in Williamsburg, Virginia. Among his primary research interests are teacher effectiveness and student success, and teacher and administrator performance evaluation. He has worked with numerous school districts, state, and national educational organizations to design and develop evaluation systems for teachers, administrators, superintendents, and support personnel. He is the author or coauthor of nineteen books and approximately ninety articles and technical reports on teacher quality, performance evaluation, and related issues. Selected authored, coauthored, and edited books include the following:

- ◆ *Student Achievement Goal Setting: Using Data to Improve Teaching and Learning* (Eye On Education, 2009)

- ◆ *Qualities of Effective Principals* (Association for Supervision and Curriculum Development, 2008)

- *Qualities of Effective Teaching, 2nd ed.* (Association for Supervision and Curriculum Development, 2007)
- *Handbook on Educational Specialist Evaluation* (Eye on Education, 2003)
- *Superintendent Evaluation Handbook* (Scarecrow Press, 2003)
- *Handbook on Teacher Evaluation* (Eye On Education, 2003)
- *Handbook on Teacher Portfolios for Evaluation and Professional Development* (Eye On Education, 2000)

His doctorate in the area of educational administration and planning was received from the University of Alabama. He has been a teacher, counselor, and district-level administrator. He can be contacted at: The College of William and Mary, School of Education, PO Box 8795, Williamsburg, VA 23187–8795; 757–221–2339; or jhstro@wm.edu.

Contents

Free Downloads

Many of the tools discussed and displayed in this book are also available on the Routledge website as Adobe Acrobat files. Permission has been granted to purchasers of this book to download these tools and print them.

You can access these downloads by visiting www.routledge.com/9781596671416 and click on the Free Downloads tab.

List of Free Downloads

Part I

Research and Practice on Teaching and Learning

1

Introduction

No doubt, the influence of individual, family, community, and other beyond-school factors dramatically influence student success. Nonetheless, of all the factors within the influence of schools, teacher quality is among the most, if not the most powerful variable affecting student achievement.[1]

As reflected in this introductory quote, we know that teacher quality matters enormously in the total scheme of schooling and student learning. In *Planning, Instruction, and Assessment: Effective Teaching Practices* our sole focus is on bridging research to practice for the fundamental issues of (1) planning and delivering effective instruction, and (2) assessing its impact on student learning. Indeed, although our profession often may view the universe of school reform at its macro level, we contend that it isn't until we get to the personalized, micro world of a teacher helping a student learn that we can really understand—and impact—reform in any meaningful manner.

This introductory chapter broaches broader issues of teacher quality as we lay the foundation for a discussion of how instructional planning, delivery, and assessment are integral to and intertwined in our most important deliverable—student learning. In particular, we address the following questions in this brief overview of the importance of teacher quality:

- ♦ What is teacher effectiveness?
- ♦ Why is teacher quality important?
- ♦ What is the relationship between teacher effectiveness and student learning?
- ♦ How is the book organized?
- ♦ How can the book be used to promote teacher quality?

What Is Teacher Effectiveness?[a]

Teacher effectiveness is a broad concept[2] that can be defined in many ways.[3] We choose to use the terms *quality* and *effectiveness* interchangeably. The word *quality* denotes the experience of being with a special teacher, whereas *effectiveness* works well when referring to analytical evidence. One clear and undeniable way to define teacher

---

[a] This section of the chapter is replicated in Chapter 1 of the Eye On Education companion book, *The Supportive Learning Environment: Effective Teaching Practices.*

effectiveness is to personally know an effective teacher, or to have benefited from the tutelage and teaching of an extraordinary teacher. Another way to define teacher effectiveness is to analyze (or dissect) it based on the extant research about what makes teachers effective. This section briefly explores both perspectives: *analyzing* an effective teacher and *interacting* with an effective teacher.

Although we may not be able to define teacher quality with precision, we certainly can identify key teacher qualities that form the foundation of any useful definition. Studies examining effective teacher characteristics are profuse and often seem to seek an elusive secret formula for teacher quality. Unfortunately, there is no single magic elixir for quality teaching. However, one thing we know for certain about teacher quality is that it is multidimensional and these multiple dimensions interact to form the chemistry of what makes good teachers good. Figure 1.1 identifies some key components of a quality teacher.[b]

Figure 1.1. Selected Characteristics of Quality Teachers

♦ *Communication skills,* including the ability to listen to and value what students have to say;[4]

♦ *Teacher preparation* in terms of content knowledge[5] and certification,[6] among others;

♦ *Personal dispositions,* such as enthusiasm, motivation, and reflectivity;[7]

♦ *Personal relationships* with students built on fairness, trust, respectfulness;[8]

♦ *Classroom management* that provides a safe, robust, disciplined, and vibrant learning environment;[9]

♦ *Instructional planning, delivery, and ongoing student assessment* combined in such a way as to constantly monitor and deliver differentiated, effective instruction;[10] and,

♦ *Clearly focused goals and high expectations* to promote student achievement.[11]

Why Is Teacher Quality Important?

Regardless of how we choose to define quality, building-level administrators and teachers know that the work of good teachers results in improvements for students, including improved instructional opportunities and improved student learning. Although we highlighted a number of key dispositions and practices (i.e., teaching processes) in the section above, let's consider the impact (i.e., results) of a high-quality teacher:

♦ Fewer discipline issues,

♦ Better relationships with their students, and, most importantly,

♦ Higher student achievement results.[12]

---

[b] For a more comprehensive review and discussion of key teacher dispositions, skills, and knowledge, see Stronge, J. H. (2007). *Qualities of effective teachers* (2nd ed.). Alexandria, VA: Association for Supervision and Curriculum Development.

Thus, any worthy definition should take into account both the *process* of teaching (e.g., quality instructional delivery skills) and the *results* of teaching (e.g., student achievement gains).

So why does teacher quality matter? Because learning matters. If we hope for our children a better quality education and a brighter tomorrow, we also must hope for— and support in every practical way—quality teachers.

What Is the Relationship Between Teacher Effectiveness and Student Learning?[c]

Analyses of data from teacher value-added assessment studies[13] offer compelling evidence regarding the influence of the classroom teacher on student learning.[14] The overarching finding from value-added studies is that effective teachers are, indeed, essential for student success. In fact, it has been estimated that out of all the factors that are within the control of schools, teachers have the greatest impact on student achievement.[15] Consider the following specific findings presented in Figure 1.2.

Figure 1.2. Teacher Impact on Student Achievement

Major Findings	Study
♦ The impact of teachers is far greater than that of overall school effects. In other words, "which teacher a student gets within a school matters more than which school the student happens to attend."	Nye, Konstantopoulos, & Hedges, 2004, (p. 247)
♦ Beginning in third grade, children placed with highly effective teachers scored on average at the 96th percentile on Tennessee's mathematics state assessment, whereas children placed with ineffective teachers scored on average at the 42nd percentile, resulting in a 52 percentile difference.	Wright, Horn, & Sanders, 1997
♦ Students of less-effective teachers experienced reading achievement gains of 1/3 standard deviation less than students with effective teachers.	Nye, Konstantopoulos, & Hedges, 2004
♦ Students of less-effective teachers experienced mathematics achievement gains of almost 1/2 standard deviation less than students with effective teachers.	Nye, Konstantopoulos, & Hedges, 2004
♦ Lower-achieving students are more likely to be placed with less-effective teachers.	Wright, Horn, & Sanders, 1997

---

[c] This section of the chapter is replicated in Chapter 1 of the Eye On Education companion book, *The Supportive Learning Environment: Effective Teaching Practices.*

♦ If a student had a high-performing teacher for just one year, the student likely would remain ahead of peers for at least the next few years of schooling (residual effect).	Mendro, 1998
♦ Third grade students of teachers in the top quartile of effectiveness (based on hierarchical linear modeling predictions) scored approximately 30–40 scale score points higher than expected on the Virginia Standards of Learning state assessment in English, Mathematics, Science, and Social Studies. Students of teachers in the bottom quartile of effectiveness scored approximately 24–32 points below expected scores.	Stronge, Tucker, & Ward, 2003
♦ The teacher has a larger effect on student achievement than any other school-related factor, including ability levels within a class and class size.	Wright, Horn, & Sanders, 1997
♦ Fifth grade students scored approximately 30 percentile points higher in both reading and mathematics in one year when assigned to top-quartile teachers as compared to those students assigned to bottom-quartile teachers.	Stronge, Ward, & Grant, 2008

To summarize the impact of effective teachers on student learning, Wright, Horn, and Sanders surmised that "seemingly more can be done to improve education by improving the effectiveness of teachers than by any other single factor."[16] Yes, we do need *highly qualified teachers* as required in the U.S. federal legislation *No Child Left Behind*. However, much more importantly, we need *high-quality* and, indeed, *highly effective* teachers.

How Is the Book Organized?

The premises of *Planning, Instruction, and Assessment: Effective Teaching Practices* are depicted in the following questions:

♦ How can teachers promote student learning through planning? *(Chapter 2)*

♦ How can teachers use research-based instructional strategies to improve student learning? *(Chapter 3)*

♦ How do teachers develop assessments and use assessment data to improve student learning? *(Chapter 4)*

♦ How can planning, instruction, and assessment be integrated into a meaningful whole in successful teachers' classrooms? *(Chapter 5)*

The Venn diagram (Figure 1.3) below depicts how *Planning, Instruction, and Assessment: Effective Teaching Practices* and its companion book, *The Supportive Learning Environment: Effective Teaching Practices* (Eye On Education, 2010), address the extant research related to teacher quality.

Figure 1.3. The Relationship Between the Companion Teacher Quality Books

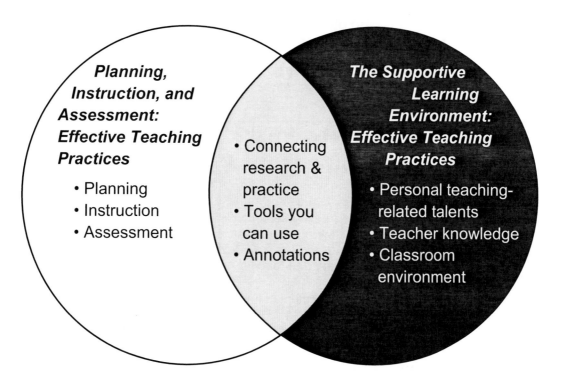

Planning, Instruction, and Assessment: Effective Teaching Practices

- Planning
- Instruction
- Assessment

- Connecting research & practice
- Tools you can use
- Annotations

The Supportive Learning Environment: Effective Teaching Practices

- Personal teaching-related talents
- Teacher knowledge
- Classroom environment

The books focus on research-based practices of teacher quality. Three parts comprise each book:

- ♦ *Part I* focuses on selected key elements that support teaching and learning, namely, instructional planning, instructional delivery, and student assessment (Chapters 1–5).

- ♦ *Part II* offers reproducible resources for use by teachers and those working with teachers.

- ♦ *Part III* includes an annotated bibliography of key publications that are related to the concepts and practice of planning, instruction, and assessment.

Figure 1.4 summarizes the relationship between the two books as they address essential elements for teacher quality.

Figure 1.4. Overview of Content for Teaching and Learning Companion Books

Chapter	*Planning, Instruction, and Assessment: Effective Teaching Practices*	*The Supportive Learning Environment: Effective Teaching Practices*
1	Teacher effectiveness defined; Impact of teacher effectiveness on student achievement	Teacher effectiveness defined; Impact of teacher effectiveness on student achievement
2	Instructional planning and teacher quality ♦ Focusing on essential knowledge and skills ♦ Differentiating instruction ♦ Using Response-to-Intervention ♦ Integrating technology effectively	Personal dispositions of quality teachers ♦ Immediacy ♦ Credibility ♦ Caring ♦ Engaging caregivers
3	Instructional delivery and teacher effectiveness ♦ Teaching for conceptual understanding ♦ Using questioning as an instructional strategy ♦ Developing inquiring minds ♦ Increasing student engagement	Professional knowledge and teacher effectiveness ♦ Certification ♦ Experience ♦ Communication ♦ Professional development ♦ Mentoring
4	Student assessment and teacher quality ♦ Developing aligned assessments ♦ Creating rubrics that communicate expectations ♦ Providing feedback ♦ Using assessment data	Teacher management skill, classroom attributes, and teacher effectiveness ♦ Learning environment ♦ Rules ♦ Routines ♦ Student ownership ♦ Time management
5	Interrelationships among planning, instruction, and assessment	Supporting teacher quality ♦ School culture ♦ Teacher reflection ♦ High expectations

How Can the Book Be Used to Promote Teacher Quality?

Effective teachers know how to use resources around them and how to maximize their own time as well as time in the classroom. *Planning, Instruction, and Assessment: Effective Teaching Practices* along with its companion book, *The Supportive Learning Envi-*

ronment: Effective Teaching Practices, focuses on those elements of education that support effective teaching and, thus, support student learning.

Our intent is that the book be a valuable resource for the following audiences:

♦ Teachers—including classroom, resource, and other settings—who desire to improve their own performance and their students' through this value-added methodology;

♦ Teacher leaders who are in a position to impact teacher practice through their support and expertise;

♦ Administrators who supervise and support teachers; and,

♦ Staff development specialists who plan and deliver training focused on improving instructional practices.

Regardless of your position in the enterprise of teaching and learning, it is our sincere hope that *Planning, Instruction, and Assessment: Effective Teaching Practices* benefits your school, your teaching practices, and, most importantly, your students.

Notes

1   Stronge, Gareis, & Little, 2006.

2   Darling-Hammond, 2008; Stronge, 2002; Stronge, 2007.

3   Yin & Kwok, 1999.

4   Darling-Hammond, 2000; Emmer, Evertson, & Anderson, 1980.

5   Felter, 1999.

6   Darling-Hammond, 2000; Darling-Hammond, Berry, & Thoreson., 2001; Goldhaber & Brewer, 2001; Hawk, Coble, & Swanson., 1985; Haycock, 2000; Miller, McKenna, & McKenna, 1998.

7   National Association of Secondary School Principals, 1997; Peart & Campbell, 1999; Stronge, 2007.

8   Marzano, Pickering, & McTighe, 1993; McBer, 2000.

9   Corbett & Wilson, 2004; Stronge, Ward, Tucker, & Hindman, 2008.

10 Marzano, 2006; Tomlinson, 1999.

11 Cotton, 2000; Johnson, 1997; Marzano, Pickering, & McTighe, 1993; Mason, Schroeter, Combs & Washington, 1992; McBer, 2000; Peart & Campbell, 1999; Shellard & Protheroe, 2000.

12 Ralph, Kesten, Lang, & Smith, 1998; Stronge, Ward, Tucker, & Hindman, 2008.

13 For an explanation and examples of teacher value-added assessment, see: Tucker & Stronge, 2005.

14 See, for example, Mendro, 1998; Nye, Konstantopoulos, & Hedges, 2004; Wright, Horn, & Sanders, 1997.

15 See, for example: Carey, 2004; Leithwood, Louis, Anderson, & Wahlstrom, 2004; Stronge, Ward, Tucker, & Hindman, 2008.

16 Wright, Horn, & Sanders, 1997, p. 63.

2

How Can Teachers Promote Student Learning Through Planning?

A professor asked a class of aspiring school administrators to define planning. Most of the students were current classroom teachers who responded with some variation that planning was a roadmap for instruction. Just as there are many types of maps, there are many types of instructional plans such as yearly, unit, weekly, and daily. However, instructional planning is more complex than a travel itinerary with an accompanying map. When traveling one has to account for weather conditions, needs of traveling companions, and a host of other considerations. These considerations and others are not taken into account on a map.

So, then, the question remains: How do teachers go about ensuring students' learning through planning? This chapter offers four distinctive ways:

♦ By focusing on essential knowledge and skills;

♦ By focusing on the individual needs of *all* students through differentiation;

♦ By using Response-To-Intervention techniques to address instructional needs; and

♦ By integrating technology for added value to the instructional process.

By Focusing on Essential Knowledge and Skills

Why Should Teachers Attend to Essential Knowledge and Skills?

> Planning is an integral part ✳ of teaching. "Pupils do notice if a teacher is ill-prepared for teaching…pupils may feel if the teacher is not prepared for teaching, why should they study hard and be accountable for doing well in school."[1] Thorough planning:
>
> ♦ Shows professionalism;[2]
>
> ♦ Demonstrates a consideration of the teaching context and students;
>
> ♦ Allows a teacher to predict possible problems and think about how to address them; and
>
> ♦ Enhances student achievement.[3]

The short-term answer to this question is to provide students with the opportunities to learn in order to be academically successful. The long-term answer to the question is to provide students with the knowledge and skills for success in life. This section of the chapter focuses on the first answer to the question—academic success. In today's era of accountability and state standards, that means a focus on the knowledge and skills that states require of their students.

Each state has now developed content standards (e.g., Florida's Sunshine State Standards) and requires that students take tests to demonstrate their proficiency.[4] In some states, these tests are high stakes for students as well as for schools. In states such as Virginia, a student's diploma may hinge on performance on an end-of-course standardized assessment.[5] In the state of Florida, a third grade student will be retained if the student fails to demonstrate proficiency on the third grade state reading assessment.[6] Consequently, teachers *must* attend to the essential knowledge and skills for their students' sake.

During the planning process, effective teachers ensure that they are preparing to teach their students the knowledge and skills that they will need to be successful not only on end-of-course assessments, but also in the next educational experience (e.g., grade, college, work training) the student encounters. In short, if students are not even exposed to the knowledge and skills that they should learn, they are surely being set up for failure. This begs the question of breadth versus depth in teaching content and skills (see sidebar for further discussion of this issue). Ensuring success begins in planning, and effective planning begins with the end in mind.

> **Breadth vs. Depth**
>
> In a study of breadth versus depth, researchers found that students in high school science courses (biology, chemistry, physics) that experienced in-depth coverage of content better prepared students for future study (i.e., performance in college science courses).[7] Conversely, breadth of coverage may result in higher standardized test scores in high school. Quite strikingly, researchers found that "Students who experience breadth of coverage in high school biology perform in college as if they had experienced half a year less preparation than students without breadth of coverage, whereas those who are exposed to in-depth coverage perform as if they had had half a year more preparation than the students without depth of coverage" (p.17).

What Does the Research Say about the Connection Between Providing Students with Essential Knowledge and Skills and Student Achievement?

Long-range or yearly lesson plans often outline the time teachers will allocate to particular standards or topics. In public schools, lesson plans are typically based on the state standards and local school system curriculum. In private schools, national subject area standards and the school curriculum typically provide the basis for these plans, including an initial overview of what students will have the opportunity to learn during the time they spend in classrooms. Figure 2.1 summarizes illustrative research studies related to the connection between focusing on essential knowledge and skills and student achievement.

Figure 2.1. Focusing on Essential Knowledge and Skills and Student Achievement

Related Findings	Citation
♦ In the first International Association of Educational Achievement study, researchers found that "a considerable amount of variation between countries in mathematics scores can be attributed to the differences between students' opportunities to learn the material which was tested."[8] In other words, whether students had been exposed to the content influenced their achievement on the test.	Husen, 1967
♦ The Third International Mathematics and Science Study (TIMSS) found that teaching in countries with higher achieving students were congruent with the learning goals of the TIMSS achievement tests. Therefore, "… it is essential to be explicit about and prioritize the learning goals."	Hiebert, et al., 2005
♦ A significant predictor of student achievement is content coverage. In other words, if essential knowledge and skills are covered in the course of classroom instruction then students will perform better.	Dunkin, 1978; Dunkin & Doenau, 1980
♦ In a study of the effects of content coverage on mathematics achievement, a team of researchers found that when factoring in both topics covered and level of depth, 20% of the difference between classes' achievement gains was explained and 7% of the difference in student achievement gains was explained. When only topic coverage was considered, the explained difference was 4% for class achievement and 1% for student achievement. Surface-level coverage of topics is not sufficient as demonstrated by this study; students need to explore topics more deeply to understand and apply them.	Gamoran, et al., 1997
♦ A study of content coverage in literacy instruction in elementary classrooms found a wide variation in coverage of reading comprehension and writing instruction among different teachers.	Rowan, Harrison, & Hayes, 2004

The sample of research studies summarized in Figure 2.1 provides evidence that, indeed, exposure to content and skills that students are expected to learn can impact student achievement and that children in different classrooms may not have access to the full curriculum. Therefore, it is incumbent on teachers that they know the essential knowledge and skills that their students must learn and translate that knowledge into interconnected daily, weekly, and yearlong planning.

How Does a Teacher Ensure That Planning Reflects Essential Knowledge and Skills?

How often have you heard a teacher say, "Yes, I taught that topic, but the students did not show what they know?" Think about a physical education teacher teaching students about tennis. The teacher could teach students the vocabulary and rules of tennis; model specific skills, such as the forehand, backhand, and crossover, and then assess students on their knowledge and acquired skills. If, however, the students are not given the opportunity to play, how can they be successful in a match? Likewise, students need the opportunity to "play ball." If they are not given the opportunity to interact with the content, and at the range of cognitive levels present in the standards, students will be ill-prepared for standards-based tests in the near-term and for life skills in the future.

Benefits of Mining State Standards

Beginning teachers would benefit from the opportunity to work closely with experienced teachers who know from prior experiences that they need to ensure that students have the requisite knowledge and skills. Experienced teachers would benefit from mining a standard because it encourages them to think about the material from the students' perspective and keeps the teachers' eyes on the goals of student learning. Teachers of varying experience levels benefit from working together as they offer to each other a diversity of instructional strategies, resources, knowledge, and content expertise. For example, if the standards were first mined and the lesson study methodology then used, teachers could work together to plan high quality instruction. In essence, the teachers "work smarter" by not duplicating each other's efforts and creating a bank of field-tested lessons complete with accommodations for different levels of learners that address the standard.

Various professional associations have developed content standards that, in turn, often are used as the basis for state standards in public education. Mining these standards holds the key to knowing what students are expected to know and be able to do. On a school or district level, teachers can work together to mine state standards for knowledge and skills expectations. By discerning what students are accountable for knowing, teachers can plan appropriately. The *Mining State Standards* template in Figure 2.2 demonstrates how a teacher unpacked a seventh grade language arts standard (a reproducible blank template of *Mining State Standards* is available in Part II). The teacher considered both the *stated expectations* and the *implied expectations* that are part of the standard.

♦ *Stated expectations* are those items that can be derived directly from the standard as it is written.

♦ *Implied expectations* are foundational knowledge and skills that students need to be successful in demonstrating competence in the standard.

A teacher reads the state standards and thinks, "What does this standard mean? What are my students expected to know and be able to do if they demonstrate achievement of this standard?" Content coverage involves both breadth and depth. In other words, not only are students expected to have knowledge and comprehension of the concepts within the standard, but also they are expected to apply, synthesize, and evaluate. Figure 2.2 provides a way to mine state standards to reach both breadth and depth. Standards contain both stated and implied expectations. For example, for stu-

Figure 2.2. Mining State Standards Example from Virginia Standards of Learning for Seventh Grade English[9]

State Standard	Content and Skills	Lower-Level Expectations (Knowledge and Comprehension)		Higher-Level Expectations (Application, Analysis, Synthesis, and Evaluation)	
		Stated	Implied	Stated	Implied
The student will read and demonstrate comprehension of a variety of fiction, narrative nonfiction, and poetry. a) Describe setting, character development, plot structure, theme, and conflict. b) Compare and contrast forms, including short stories, novels, plays, folk literature, poetry, essays, and biographies. c) Describe the impact of word choice, imagery, and poetic devices. d) Explain how form, including rhyme, rhythm, repetition, line structure, and punctuation, conveys the mood and meaning of a poem. e) Draw conclusions based on explicit and implied information. f) Make inferences based on explicit and implied information. g) Summarize text.	*Content:* Fiction Narrative nonfiction Poetry *Skills:* Ability to read and decode text Use context clues Use graphic organizers Use story maps	Understand elements of a story (setting, plot, theme, character, internal conflict, external conflict) Recognize poetic devices (rhyme, rhythm, repetition)	Understand relationship between elements in the writing, characterization, foreshadowing, irony, and how authors make choices to create a story Recognize poetic devices (meter, alliteration, assonance, consonance, onomatopoeia) Identify haiku, limerick, ballad, free verse, couplet, quatrain, voice, and mood	Make inferences Make conclusions	Analyze author's style (word choice, figurative language) Differentiate between short stories, novels, folk literature, plays, personal essays, biographies, autobiographies Begin to analyze text Compare/contrast narrative and poetic forms

dents to be able to understand elements of a story, they must also understand the relationship between these elements in the writing such as characterization, foreshadowing and irony. In order for students to make inferences, they must be able to analyze the author's style of writing and understand figurative language. Teachers can use this preplanning tool to identify expectations, then they can begin to think about appropriate instructional activities and classroom-based assessments given the expectations contained within the standard. Most importantly, however, the teacher has a clear sense of what students are expected to know and be able to do, and to plan accordingly.

By Focusing on the Individual Needs of *All* Students through Differentiation

What is Differentiation?

Differentiation is a hot topic in educational circles. Attend any local, state, or national conferences on teaching and learning, and most likely you will find numerous presentations on this very topic. Although differentiation traditionally has been associated with gifted education, the concept has now entered the mainstream of education. In fact, much of the research and strategies developed to meet the needs of gifted students have been adopted by school districts to meet the needs of all students.[10] So, what is differentiation, and what must teachers know and be able to do in order to use this valuable strategy? Essentially, "differentiation is modified instruction that helps students with diverse academic needs and learning styles master the same challenging content."[11]

What Does Research Say About the Connection Between Differentiation and Student Learning?

The research on the impact of differentiation on student learning is replete with studies that focus on the elements of differentiation. These elements include differentiation based on academic readiness, student interest, and student learning preferences.[12] Tomlinson and colleagues reviewed the research literature related to these three areas. Figure 2.3 summarizes their findings.

What Do Teachers Need to Know in Order to Differentiate?

To successfully differentiate instruction, a teacher needs to have a set of fundamental skills and knowledge. These include:

♦ Knowing students,

♦ Knowing the curriculum,

♦ Knowing available resources

♦ Knowing sound assessment practices, and

♦ Knowing a range of effective instructional strategies.

**Figure 2.3. Research Literature Review
Findings Related to Differentiation[13]**

Areas Related to Differentiation	Research Literature Review Findings
	Evidence supports that…
Academic Readiness	◆ Students perform better when academic tasks are neither too easy nor too difficult. In other words, they are just right. ◆ Students in multiage or nongraded classrooms perform better than students in single-age or graded classrooms.
Student Interest	◆ Students who enjoy learning tend to seek continued learning experiences. ◆ Students who are interested in what they are learning tend to feel more able to complete tasks, accept challenges, and continue to work on a challenge.
Student Learning Profile	◆ Students at all school levels, regardless of gender or ethnic background, perform better academically when instructional activities are matched to their learning style. ◆ Students who are aware of their own learning preferences can take advantage of this knowledge by "capitalizing on their strengths and weaknesses."[14]

Know Your Students

Knowing the needs and interests of students is at the heart of differentiation, and of good teaching, for that matter. The root word of "differentiation" is "different." Each student comes to the classroom with his own set of experiences, skills, and knowledge, which are unique from classmates' academic, practical, and tacit knowledge base. Knowing students involves knowing their academic needs, individual interests, and learning preferences.[15] (See the sidebar regarding ways to assess student interests and learning preferences on page 18.) This may be accomplished through the use of preassessment of knowledge and skills, interest inventories, and learning styles inventories.

Know the Curriculum

The curriculum forms the basis for differentiation, along with student needs and interests. Effective teachers know the content and skills that students should master after spending a year in their classroom. They not only know mathematics, for example, but also they know many ways to teach it. In other words, they have the content knowledge as well as the pedagogical content knowledge. These two elements are essential aspects of effective teaching,[17] and essential for effective differentiation.[18]

Know Available Resources

Resources are another critical component for differentiated instruction as teachers plan for a variety of activities. Resources may include texts written at varying reading levels and other print media, technology tools, manipulatives, and visuals to enhance varying levels of understanding. Selecting the appropriate resources to use with students is a critical component in addition to knowing about available resources.[19]

Know How to Assess Effectively

Differentiated instruction calls for multiple modes of assessing student learning.[20] In other words, students should have multiple options in demonstrating what they have learned. To do that, a teacher must have the basic skill of being able to assess minute-by-minute, day-by-day, week-by-week, and year-by-year. In fact, it has been predicted that when a teacher's skill in formative assessment increases, student achievement increases.[21] Assessments may include standardized assessments used to monitor progress in early literacy skills as well as performance-based assessments accompanied by a valid rubric that is based on what students should know and be able to do.

Know a Range of Instructional Strategies and How to Implement Them Successfully

Effective teachers have a repertoire of instructional strategies for working with students.[22] They use learning centers, tiered activities, anchor activities, problem-based learning, questioning, and a host of others.[23] The effectiveness of the teacher in the act of teaching is described as a "nonnegotiable" in delivering quality gifted programs.[24] However, having a teacher who is effective is critical for any student, in any classroom.

How Does a Teacher Differentiate a Lesson for the Diverse Group of Learners in the Classroom?

One way to differentiate instruction is to provide options based on student understanding of the concepts being studied and student interest in the concept, or learning profile. This strategy is typically referred to as "tiered lessons." Tomlinson and Eidson define tiering as "a process of adjusting the degree of difficulty of a question, task, or product to match a student's current readiness level."[25]

Researchers working in a laboratory school developed tiered lessons and shared their insights on how to develop a tiered lesson effectively and described how a lesson can be tiered based on not only readiness level, but on interest and learning styles.[26] Essentially, eight steps are involved in creating a tiered lesson. Steps 1 to 4 set the stage for the lesson, in step 5 the teacher begins the process of articulating how the lesson will be tiered, which continues through step 8. Figure 2.4 describes these steps.

Figure 2.4. Steps in Developing a Tiered Lesson[27]

Step	Description
Step 1: What grade level or subject will be the focus of the lesson?	This is the first big step in creating a tiered lesson. The grade level and subject provide the focus for the lesson and determine the content and the developmental level at which the lesson will be taught.
Step 2: What standard will be the focus of the lesson?	The standards may include state standards, district curriculum standards, or national standards for the subject being taught. The standards provide the specific aspect of the subject that will be the focus and delineate exactly what students should know and be able to do by the end of the lesson.
Step 3: What key concepts and generalizations should students learn from the lesson?	The teacher steps back and thinks about the big concept or "big idea" that students should learn by the end of the lesson. This is a critical component, as learning should involve meaningful connections rather than a study of isolated information or facts.
Step 4: What prerequisite knowledge or skills do students have or not have to be successful with the lesson?	The teacher breaks down the concept and skills by thinking about what students need to know or be able to do in order to engage with the key concepts, generalizations, and standards. In other words, what has the teacher already taught and what might she still need to teach before engaging in the tiered lesson?
Step 5: What part of the lesson will be tiered?	Different parts of the lesson can be tiered—the delivery of the content, how students engage with the content, or the product of their learning. The researchers recommend that a novice at differentiation tier only one aspect of a lesson.
Step 6: How will the lesson be tiered?	The teacher decides the basis for the tiering. For example, lessons may be tiered based on student readiness, in which case the teacher must be able to formatively assess student understanding and determine readiness. Student interest and learning profile are other ways in which lessons may be tiered. The researchers recommend using student interest surveys or learning styles inventories for these last two options.

Step 7: How many tiers will be needed?	Deciding how a lesson will be tiered will help determine how many levels will be part of the lesson. If the lesson will be tiered based on student readiness, then levels may include limited understanding of concept, understanding of concept, and thorough understanding of concept. A tiered lesson based on interests or learning style, in turn, may include a limited number of choices from which students may choose, such as selected readings, hands-on activity, or acting out a skit.
Step 8: How will students be assessed?	The nature of the part of the lesson that will be tiered will help determine how students will be assessed. If the process in the lesson will be tiered, then the most appropriate type of assessment may be formative, such as teacher observations of student learning. If the product of the lesson will be tiered, on the other hand, perhaps summative assessment will be most effective.

The researchers cautioned that regardless of the lessons that are tiered, all activities must be meaningful and challenging for each student. As teachers gain experience with tiering, the more confident they will become in using this differentiation strategy. Tiering is truly data-driven instruction as the tiering is based on student abilities, interests, and/or talents.

To illustrate the use of tiered lessons, a sample science lesson plan is provided in the *Tiered Lesson Plan Template* (Figure 2.5) with the accompanying activity sheet (Figure 2.6, page 22) that the students would complete (a blank reproducible copy of the *Tiered Lesson Plan Template* is provided in Part II). In this case, the process and the product are tiered. The process is the same for the first two tiers: Students will be using a specific procedure to complete the lab. However, in the third tier, students write their own procedure. Notice that each tier has students engaged with the content in a meaningful, but appropriate way. One of the cautions in using tiered lessons is to make sure that each tier is engaging. How disappointing to a group of students when they are completing a workshop while another group is conducting a "cool" experiment. The product in the sample is tiered for all three groups.

Figure 2.5. Sample Tiered Lesson Plan Template

Teacher: Mr. Redd	**Grade Level/Subject:** 5th Grade Science
Topic: Scientific Investigations	

Local, State, or National Standard: Design and conduct a scientific investigation

Essential Understanding(s): Parts of an experiment, laboratory safety, metric measurement

Type of Differentiation: ☒ Academic readiness, based on student ability to design and execute an investigation. ☐ Student interest, based on _____ ☐ Learning preference, based on _____	**Portion of Lesson Tiered:** ☐ Content ☒ Process ☒ Product

Lesson Description: Review the experimental design diagram. Inform students that there will be a lab involving metric measurement in which they will have to construct rockets and change an aspect related to the rocket fins in order to see how to make the rocket go farther. Review applicable lab safety rules.

Teacher-Provided Materials: Meter stick, scissors, paper, straws, direction page for rocket building, and differentiated activity sheets

Tiered Element Description:

Tier 1—Verification lab with word bank provided for students whose preassessment indicated little to no knowledge of variables and constants.

Tier 2—Verification lab (most of the class) for students with either (a) limited lab skills or (b) no proficiency in identifying the parts of an experiment, including variables and constants.

Tier 3—Guided inquiry for students who have demonstrated proficiency in conducting verification labs. These students have a question in which they will need to determine what about the fins (e.g., position, shape, paper type) will be changed. Their instruction sheet contains only information for constructing the initial rocket body and launching instructions related to safety. The group will need to determine some elements of the procedure that will be used.

Assessment: Completion of the experimental design diagram handout; teacher observation of lab safety

Figure 2.6. Sample Student Activity Sheets

**Verification Lab:
Experimental Design Diagram**

Word Bank	ruler disease	fin position paper	straw go farther	tape

Title: *The effect of fins on rocket flight.*

Hypothesis: If the _____ is moved then rocket will _____

Independent variable (what is changed): _____

Dependent variable (what is observed): _____

Constants (what stays the same): _____

	Rocket with rear fins	Rocket with front fins	Control—rocket with no fins
Trial 1			
Trial 2			
Trial 3			

Experimental Design Diagram from Cothron, Giese, & Rezba, 1989.

**Verification Lab:
Experimental Design Diagram**

Title: *The effect of fins on rocket flight.*

Hypothesis: *If the _____ is moved then rocket will _____*

Independent variable (what is changed): _____

Dependent variable (what is observed): _____

Constants (what stays the same): _____

	Control—rocket with no fins	Rocket with rear fins	Rocket with front fins
Trial 1			
Trial 2			
Trial 3			

Experimental Design Diagram from Cothron, Giese, & Rezba, 1989.

Quided Inquiry:
Experimental Design Diagram

Question:

       What is the best fin design on a rocket to get it to fly the farthest?

Title: _____

Hypothesis: _____

Independent variable (what is changed): _____

Dependent variable (what is observed): _____

Constants (what stays the same): _____

Trial 1			
Trial 2			
Trial 3			

Experimental Design Diagram from Cothron, Giese, & Rezba, 1989.

By Using Response-To-Intervention to Address Instructional Needs[a]

What is Response-To-Intervention?

Response-To-Intervention (RtI), is a general education process or model whereby a student is provided supplemental or more intensive intervention based upon the identification of an academic, social, or behavioral challenge. Throughout the multitiered intervention process, the intensity of the student's intervention is adjusted and redesigned, as needed, as the student's response to that intervention is continuously and consistently monitored and assessed.[28] At the conclusion of the process, improvements may warrant that the student be removed from the supplemental intervention. In other instances, where documented monitoring supports little to no academic, social, or behavioral improvements, it may be determined that a referral for a special education evaluation is needed.

"True" or "real" learning disabilities are permanent and are evidenced by identified cognitive deficits.[29] The RtI process focuses primarily on problem solving via the manipulation of instruction and the school environment. Through the use of RtI, intervention is focused on those controllable aspects of student learning (i.e., the external environment). The teacher identifies student at-risk behaviors, provides prereferral interventions, and may rule out those external factors as being the cause of the student learning deficits, thus providing additional evidence to support the need for a referral to special education. Figure 2.7 provides an overview of the RtI process.

Curriculum-Based Measurement 101

Curriculum-based measurement (CBM) is a method of measuring student academic, behavioral, and social progress through direct assessment of identified skills.[30] With CBM, the teacher creates an "assessment system" used with the entire classroom specifically to track student response to instruction. Individual student academic, behavioral, and social growth may be measured with CBM and compared with both individual and classroom baseline scores and anticipated benchmarks. Applied in different phases of intervention, CBM is used to collect initial baseline data, and then, as instruction is modified reflective of individual student need, CBM is used again to measure student progress as a result of the modified instruction. Ultimately, the data collected through the multiple phases of the RtI process provides the teacher with essential information needed to modify instruction as well as that data needed to determine if a student is actually learning from what is being taught.

---

[a] This section was contributed by Patricia J. McMahon, Ph.D.

Figure 2.7. Components of a RtI Model

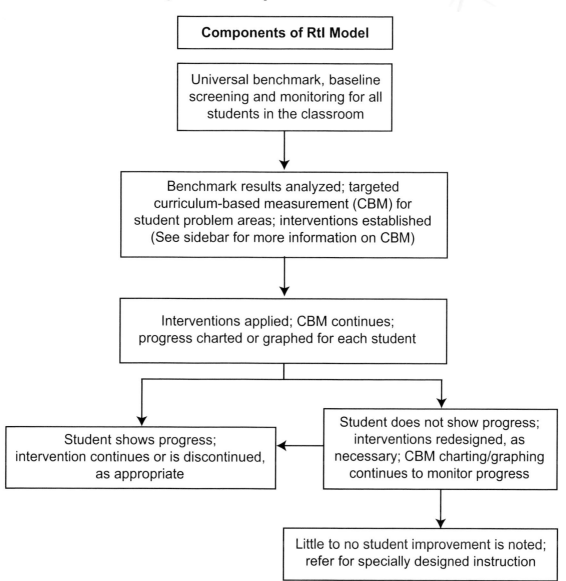

Components of RtI Model

Universal benchmark, baseline screening and monitoring for all students in the classroom

Benchmark results analyzed; targeted curriculum-based measurement (CBM) for student problem areas; interventions established (See sidebar for more information on CBM)

Interventions applied; CBM continues; progress charted or graphed for each student

Student shows progress; intervention continues or is discontinued, as appropriate

Student does not show progress; interventions redesigned, as necessary; CBM charting/graphing continues to monitor progress

Little to no student improvement is noted; refer for specially designed instruction

What Does Research Say About the Connection Between Response-To-Intervention and Student Learning?

Response-to-Intervention is relatively new on the educational scene. First defined in 1982[32] and more visible in research and practice over the last 10 years,[33] RtI remains a mysterious practice for many educators. The elements contained within RtI are supported by research, although research on the comprehensive RtI process in unclear. Consider the selected research findings related to elements of RtI provided in Figure 2.8.

Figure 2.8. Elements of RtI and Related Research Findings

Element of RtI	Related Findings	Citation(s)
◆ Supplemental instruction/intensive intervention	◆ Studies have consistently shown that students who receive supplemental instruction and/or intensive intervention demonstrate some improvement.	Baton-Arwood, Wehby, & Falk, 2005; Batsche et al., 2006; Fuchs, Fuchs, & Compton, 2004; Speech, Case, & Malloy, 2003
◆ Identifying needs	◆ RtI is instrumental in identifying students with reading disabilities in the general education classroom and results in continued progress in reading ability among students.	Vaughn, Linan-Thompson, & Hickman, 2003
◆ Progress monitoring	◆ In a study of teachers' use of Accelerated Math and continuous progress monitoring, the researchers found that students whose teachers used continuous progress monitoring significantly outperformed the students in control conditions.	Yesseldyke & Bolt, 2007
◆ Data use in modifying instruction	◆ In a review of studies examining the effects of progress monitoring on student achievement, progress monitoring data alone did not appear to affect achievement. Students realized significant gains when teachers responded to the continuous progress monitoring database by tailoring the instructional program to student needs.	Yesseldyke & Bolt, 2007

Identification of needs, the provision of supplemental instruction, implementation of interventions, and close progress monitoring support increased student achievement. Each of these elements is essential to Response-To-Intervention.

Why Should Teachers Engage in the RtI Problem-Solving Approach When Planning for Instruction?

The simplest answer to this question is to provide adequate instruction so that teachers can meet the needs of individual students within the general education setting. *Adequate instruction* is high-quality general education instruction that is matched to student needs.[34] Simply put, the best instructional strategy is the one that works. Before determining that a strategy "works," however, there must be evidence from student learning (i.e., continuous monitoring and evaluation) to support the determination.

Aren't educators already doing this? To some degree, yes. Classroom teachers keep grade books and document scores from school-, district-, and state-mandated assessments. Cumulative student records document a running history of Child Study meetings, End-of-Course and other standardized tests, and referrals for school-based services. Teachers are provided training on how to differentiate instruction to meet the needs of all students, and when students do not meet the benchmark, referrals for special education are made.

Are teachers and administrators doing enough? The demand to eliminate the achievement gap among our students remains an obligatory, yet daunting assignment. The *Individuals with Disabilities Education Act* (IDEA, 2004) requires documentation that a student has received adequate general education instruction prior to determining that the child has an identified learning disability. Additionally, IDEA requires that students with disabilities receive their education in the general education setting as the *default* and that research-based practices are used in instruction. It is only after evidence supports that a student cannot benefit from the general education setting that alternative settings and instruction are to be tried.

Including the RtI process at the school level requires a paradigm shift among educational professionals, but the resulting early intervention, enhanced student outcomes, and eliminating the wait-to-fail model in education will make the change much worth the effort.[35] The RtI process produces and includes that data and results to support whether or not adequate, quality instruction is being provided.

How Does a Teacher Plan for the RtI Process?

Tiered levels of support are suggested to be included as part of the intervention process. Research shows that it is likely most students identified as being "at risk" for academic, behavioral, and social challenges will respond to scientifically based instruction, and it is imperative that teachers implement a process whereby student skill deficits are identified, analyzed, and remediated. Figure 2.9 offers a systematic approach to the process. In fact, Figure 2.9 illustrates a problem-solving approach for individual students, using a multitiered intervention process for identifying the problem and tracking results. Each of these steps in the process is described in the following paragraphs.

Figure 2.9. Steps in the RtI Process

```
┌─────────────────────────────────────┐
│            Step 1:                   │
│   Monitor Whole-Class Progress       │
└─────────────────────────────────────┘
                 │
                 ▼
┌─────────────────────────────────────┐
│            Step 2:                   │
│        Identify the Problem          │
└─────────────────────────────────────┘
                 │
                 ▼
┌─────────────────────────────────────┐
│            Step 3:                   │
│         Develop the Plan             │
└─────────────────────────────────────┘
                 │
                 ▼
┌─────────────────────────────────────┐
│            Step 4:                   │◄──┐
│        Implement the Plan            │   │
└─────────────────────────────────────┘   │
                 │                         │
                 ▼                         │
┌─────────────────────────────────────┐   │
│            Step 5:                   │   │
│         Evaluate the Plan            │   │
└─────────────────────────────────────┘   │
                 │                         │
                 ▼                         │
┌─────────────────────────────────────┐   │
│            Step 6:                   │   │
│    Redesign or Modify the Plan       │───┘
└─────────────────────────────────────┘
```

Step 1: Whole-Class Progress Monitoring

At the beginning of the RtI process the teacher collects data using a universal screening tool for all students within the classroom. The district may require a districtwide benchmark, screening, or other curriculum-based or criterion-referenced test, and these assessments are typically given three or four times per year. It may be appropriate to use these results as the universal benchmark for your class, and these results will often provide appropriate progress monitoring data for most students.

Step 2: Identify the Problem

The next step in the process is to analyze the results of the classroom-wide screening to determine problem areas for particular students. It is appropriate to conduct a second tier of assessment for these students using a screening instrument designed specifically for the identified deficit area of the individual student. Within this process, the learning *problem* is identified. For example, if a student demonstrates difficulty with basic addition problems, the student should be assessed again with a curriculum-based assessment (CBM—see sidebar earlier in the chapter) designed for basic math skills. Teachers should be thorough in observations of the student during other tasks, times of day, and so forth, seeking to determine if the student responds differently at a different time of day or when working with fewer distractions, less noise, smaller groups, etc. The additional results obtained from this second tier of assessment become the baseline for the individual student.

Step 3: Develop a Plan

The next step in the problem-solving model is to develop of *plan of action* for the class and for the individual students. Based upon the results of the whole-class and individual assessments, the teacher may conclude that the general education instruction with some differentiation will meet the needs of all students. For those students who do not meet the identified norm, however, a more intensive, supplemental, or different instructional approach may be required. These students will require a plan of action that includes a greater intensity of instruction that will produce the identified outcome: to improve or remedy the identified deficit skill.

Step 4: Implement the Plan

Following the identification of the problem and the designing of a plan to remediate the problem, the teacher implements the designed instruction or intervention (i.e., the *plan*). Documentation of the student's response to the intervention provides evidence of progress or lack of progress for the student. Various data collection strategies (e.g., charts, graphs, narrative reports) are employed. The progress schedule (i.e., length of time and instructional intensity of the strategy) is reflective of student progress. If the child responds, the evidence supports that the intervention is working; if the child fails to respond, the intervention should be intensified with monitoring of progress continued.

Step 5: Evaluate, Evaluate, Evaluate

Using CBM, teachers will have specific student data to indicate whether progress is being made. The RtI approach supports multiple tiers of assessment and intervention. Instead of deciding to discontinue (or continue) a strategy of instruction after a defined period of time, teachers should look to the evidence shown by the student data.[36] If the student is improving, continue the strategy. If not, modify or change the strategy to address the identified need.

Step 6: Redesign or Modify the Plan

Periodically compare the collected data to the student's baseline information. Using this information, determine if the instruction or intervention has been effective. If effective, determine if the intervention may be discontinued or if it needs to continue for an additional length of time. If ineffective, the teacher should redesign and/or modify the strategy and intervention reflective of the data collected. After the intervention is implemented and the results of the plan evaluated, should little to no student progress be noted, the next tier or level of intervention (i.e., services from a school-based specialist or referral for special education evaluation) may be warranted. Again, the intensity of the intervention and the length of time the intervention is provided must be directed by student performance data. If the student is improving, the intervention is working.

Collecting & Documenting Data with the Form

The *Student Progress Monitoring Summary* template (Figure 2.10, page 31) may be used by teachers as a tool for collecting evidence for tracking student progress. Teachers may wish to add graphs and charts created electronically or on standard graph paper (a blank reproducible of the *Student Progress Monitoring Summary* template is available in Part II). The form and attached graphs may be presented to parents at parent–teacher conferences or at team meetings (i.e., Student Assistance Team or Child Study) where an individual student's progress is discussed. The form also may be used at these meetings in order to include members from multi-disciplinary teams in the brainstorming and problem-solving process, in other words to plan for future instruction and interventions.

By Integrating Technology for Added Value to Teaching and Learning

Why Should Teachers Consider Technology Options When Planning for Instruction?

Before considering this question, consider the term *technology integration*. One definition of this term is "the pervasive and productive use of education technologies for purposes of curriculum-based teaching and learning."[37] Notice that this definition does *not* provide support for use of technology for technology's sake. It does, however, support the notion that the use of technology is likened to choosing appropriate instructional resources to support learning in the classroom.[38] In other words, technology is used to support the curriculum. And so, this section does not provide a plethora of technology resources that are available for use in the K-12 classroom, but rather places technology integration in the context of planning to meet curricular and student needs.

One innovative way to think about the integration of technology has emerged through the development of a framework called Technological Pedagogical Content Knowledge or TPCK.[39] Essentially, TPCK posits that teachers need to know the interrelationships of various types of teaching and learning knowledge for successful technology integration. These types of knowledge, building on each other, are included in Figure 2.11 (page 32).

Figure 2.10. Student Progress Monitoring Summary Template

School: _____ Grade: _____

Student Name: _____

Teacher: _____ Student Monitoring Initiation Date: _____

Student Skill Deficit or Challenge being monitored: _____

Criteria for Success (i.e., at what point will intervention be discontinued?) _____

This part of the chart is from Step 1 of the process. Analyzing scores from whole-class assessment provides the teacher with baseline data.

Student Baseline/Benchmark Data and Progress Scores from Whole-Class Assessment

School-/Districtwide Tool	First Screening Date/Score	Second Screening Date/Score	Third Screening Date/Score	Fourth Screening Date/Score

Interventions Provided to Address Identified Skill Deficit Above:

Intervention Description	Start Date	End Date	Criterion Met?

Interventions include instructional strategies that will address the area of need for the student.

Individual Student Curriculum-Based Measurement (CBM) Results:

CBM Used	Date/Score	Date/Score	Date/Score	Date/Score	Date/Score	Date/Score

CBM includes the assessments used to monitor student progress. Interventions can then be modified to move student learning forward.

Student Progress Monitoring Completion Date (if applicable): _____

Use the back of this form for narrative progress notes and additional attached sheets for charts and graphs of CBM scores.

Figure 2.11. Types of Knowledge in TPCK

Type of Knowledge	What Teachers Need to Know...
Content	The subject matter they teach.
Pedagogical Content	How to teach the subject matter.
Technological Pedagogical Content	The technologies that support the pedagogy as well as the subject matter that they teach.

How many professional development sessions focus on helping teachers use technology that has just been installed in the classroom? Often this professional development teaches teachers how to use the technology, but the uses are considered outside of the realm of the content that teachers teach or instructional strategies they may use to best teach the content. With the TPCK model, technology is supportive of the curriculum, rather than a focal point of the curriculum. During planning the teacher considers first the curriculum, the pedagogy, and then the technology tools and resources that are available.

What Does Research Say About the Connection Between Technology and Student Learning?

The focus on the connection between the use of technology and student achievement began in the late 1990s and so the research is still in its infancy.[40] Researchers have set out to examine this connection and Figure 2.12 (page 33) offers a sample of research related to technology and student learning. From these studies, we conclude that technology, then, is a tool to meet the needs of the curriculum and the students and should be a factor in a teacher's decision of how to do just that. Rather than the driver, the technology is the support.

How Does a Teacher Plan for Technology Integration?

Based on TPCK's development and the research related to how technology supports teaching and learning, a teacher can use the following steps to ensure that technology is used in a supportive, thoughtful way rather than an erratic, "neat thing to do" way.

♦ *Step 1*—Unpack the curriculum for both content and thinking level required.

♦ *Step 2*—Decide on the most appropriate instructional strategies and/or models to use when teaching that content at the appropriate thinking level.

♦ *Step 3*—Consider the technology resources available to support both the content, cognitive level, and the instructional strategies.

♦ *Step 4*—Decide on the technology resource(s) that will best support student learning of the essential knowledge and skills identified in Step 1.

Figure 2.12. Sample Studies Focusing on Technology Integration and Student Achievement

Related Findings	Citation
◆ A review of the research in 1999 related to the impact of technology found that when students had access to technologies they showed achievement gains. However, the use of technology did not result in student achievement gains when the learning goals were ambiguous or unclear or when its use was erratic and unfocused.	Schacter, 1999
◆ The impact of technology use on student achievement is predicated on whether the use of the technology supports curricular aims. In other words, teachers did not use technology because it was "a neat thing to show students" but used technology to support the curriculum.	Cradler, McNabb, Freeman, & Burchett, 2002
◆ The use of technology can encourage the development of critical thinking skills in students.	Cradler, McNabb, Freeman, & Burchett, 2002
◆ Technology use in the classroom prepares students for post-high school challenges, whether entering the world of work or continuing education.	Cradler, McNabb, Freeman, & Burchett, 2002
◆ Researchers examined the relationship between technology use and student achievement on the National Assessment of Educational Progress (NAEP). Their findings suggest that frequency of technology use was negligible in impacting student achievement and, in fact, overuse was counterproductive to the learning process. What mattered was *how* teachers used technology in the classroom. When teachers used technology to teach higher-order concepts, students performed better on the NAEP. The effectiveness of the use of technology was related to the curriculum.	Wenglinsky, 1998

Although these steps offer a linear process for planning and the integration of technology, we know that the planning process is often nonlinear in that each step is actually considered simultaneously. The resulting process is synergistic, more like a web than a staircase. With that said, a novice teacher often needs a staircase in order to later begin building their own webs as they become more experienced and therefore aware of connections.

Figure 2.13 provides an example of a teacher's thought process in planning for United States History by integrating content, pedagogy, and technology. The teacher used the reproducible resource to consider what to teach and how to teach (A blank reproducible copy of this resource is available in Part II). The top row provides the overall standards that the students are expected to know and be able to do.

Figure 2.13. Steps in Planning for Instruction to Include Technology Integration

Standards:
◆ Demonstrate knowledge of the effects of World War II on the home front by describing the contributions of women and minorities in the war effort.
◆ Identify, analyze, and interpret primary and secondary source documents
◆ Formulate historical questions and defend findings based on inquiry and interpretation.[41]

Step 1: Unpack the curriculum for content and cognitive level	Knowledge	Comprehension	Application	Analysis	Synthesis	Evaluation	Step 2: Choose an Appropriate Instructional Strategy	Step 3: Examine Technology Tools Available	Step 4: Decide on the most appropriate technology tool to use with curriculum and instructional strategy
Content: ◆ effects of World War II on the home front	X	X		X			Possible Strategies: ◆ Lecture with discussion ◆ Debate ◆ Generating and testing hypotheses	Internet Access Presentation Tools	National Archives Historical Database of Primary and Secondary Documents[42]
◆ contributions of women and minorities in the war effort	X	X							
◆ primary and secondary source documents		X	X	X			Chosen Strategy: Generating and testing hypotheses		
◆ historical questions and findings based on historical analysis and interpretation					X	X			

The teacher methodically considered each element related to TPCK, including the content, the pedagogy, and the technology tools. A further description of the teacher's thoughts regarding each step of the process is provided below:

◆ *Step 1*—The content contained within these learning goals are as follows: effects of World War II on the home front, contributions of women and minorities in the war effort. They will come to this understanding through primary and secondary source documents. The thinking levels required here are at the range of Bloom's taxonomy to include knowledge, comprehension, application, analysis, synthesis, and evaluation.

♦ *Step 2*—The history teacher reviews the content and cognitive processes and decides on the research-based instructional strategy of generating and testing hypotheses.[43] In this strategy students identify an issue, generate hypotheses regarding the issue, and investigate to prove or disprove the hypotheses. In this case the teacher will set up the learning experience so that students are investigating the contributions of minorities and women to the World War II effort. This instructional strategy is appropriate for both the content and the cognitive level.

♦ *Step 3*—The teacher considers the technology resources available. He has Internet access available as well as various presentation tools.

♦ *Step 4*—The teacher decides to place the students in groups, search the Internet for historical documents related to that time period, and use the documents as evidence to be provided to test hypotheses.

In this scenario, the United States History teacher has let the curriculum dictate what and how technology will be integrated rather than the other way around.

Summary

Planning is the start to any successful endeavor and is critical to ensuring that all students learn. The planning process is complex and multifaceted taking into account both curriculum needs and student needs. On top of that, a teacher also needs to consider the resources and materials that will support and enhance the students' learning experiences. This chapter provides four ways to thoughtfully and intentionally plan for student learning. These include:

♦ Beginning with the end in mind by focusing on knowledge and skills that students must know and be able to do;

♦ Planning instruction to meet the needs of students whether based on academic readiness, interest, or learning preferences;

♦ Planning interventions for students in the general education classroom through Response-To-Intervention; and

♦ Integrating technology in a way that supports curriculum.

Notes

1   Ediger, 2004.

2   Robertson, & Acklam, 2000.

3   Duff, n.d.

4   Education Week, 2008.

5   Virginia Department of Education, 2006.

6   Florida Department of Education, 2007.

7   Schwartz, Sadler, Sonnert, & Tai, 2009.

8   Husen, 1967, p. 169.

9   Virginia Department of Education, 2003.

10 VanTassel-Baska, 2005.

11 The Center for Comprehensive School Reform and Improvement, 2007.

12 Tomlinson, 2000.

13 Tomlinson & Eidson, 2003.

14 Tomlinson & Eidson, 2003, p. 8.

15 Pierce, & Adams, 2004.

16 Gardner, 1993.

17 Stronge, 2007.

18 Carolan & Guinn, 2007.

19 The Center for Comprehensive School Reform and Improvement, 2007; VanTassel-Baska, 2005.

20 VanTassel-Baska, 2005; The Center for Comprehensive School Reform and Improvement, 2007.

21 Marzano, 2006.

22 Stronge, 2007.

23 Tomlinson, 1999; The Center for Comprehensive School Reform and Improvement, 2007; VanTassel-Baska, 2005.

24 VanTassel-Baska, 2005.

25 Tomlinson, & Eidson, 2003, p. 239.

26 Pierce & Adams, 2004.

27 Pierce & Adams, 2004.

28 Batsche et al., 2006.

29 Vaughn & Fuchs, 2003, p. 142.

30 Vaughn & Fuchs, 2003.

31 Stecker & Lembke, 2005.

32 Vaughn & Fuchs, 2003.

33 Batsche et al., 2006.

34 Batsche et al., 2006.

35 Wisconsin DPI, 2006; Vaughn & Fuchs, 2003.

36 Batsche et al., 2006.

37 Harris, 2007.

38 J. B. Harris, personal communication, November 15, 2008.

39 Mishra, & Koehler, 2006.

40 Schacter, 1999.

41 Virginia Department of Education, 2008.

42 U.S. National Archives and National Administration, http://www.archives.gov/ is an online warehouse of historical documents and records.

43 Marzano, Pickering, & Pollock, 2001.

3

How Can Teachers Use Research-Based Instructional Strategies to Improve Student Learning?

Instruction is the act of teaching—the implementation of detailed, engaging lesson plans developed in the teacher's mind and brought to life in the classroom. Curriculum guides, daily lesson plans, long-range lesson plans are merely documents on a shelf until they actually come into contact with a student. The medium through which that contact takes place is the teacher. Ultimately, the teacher chooses the strategies and resources and decides how students will be grouped for instruction.

Through research we now have the confidence to say that some teachers are better at the art and science of teaching than others. Chapter 1 detailed research studies supporting this important point that those of us in education have known all along—the interaction between the teacher and the student can lead to either increased student learning, flat student learning, or decreased student learning.[1] Although the work teachers do outside the classroom to get ready for instruction certainly play a role in success, it is the impact of the teacher on the student during instruction that seals the deal.

But, the question still remains: How can teachers use research-based instructional strategies to improve student learning? This chapter focuses on specific ways to improve student learning through the instructional act, including:

- ◆ By teaching for conceptual understanding

- ◆ By using questioning as an instructional strategy

- ◆ By developing inquiring minds

- ◆ By increasing student engagement through challenging instruction

By Teaching for Conceptual Understanding

Why Should Teachers Focus on Conceptual Understanding?

Teachers should focus on conceptual understanding because students learn better and remember more when they can connect information to their existing understandings and then relate to information in meaningful ways.[2] Teaching facts in isolation and the practice of *drill and kill*, on the other hand, ensures that students can define words, provide lists, and remember certain dates and events. Unfortunately, a student can memorize a term and never fully understand the concept behind a term. Consider, for example, the concept of fractions in mathematics. A student can memorize what a fraction is and can probably, in fact, carry out procedures to add or subtract fractions. However, unless the student has a conceptual understanding of the meaning behind a fraction, the student will encounter novel situations involving fractions and may not be able to transfer that learning.

This is not to say that facts are not important. Facts can help build the foundation for understanding concepts. But just as facts are important, so are ideas, theories, perceptions, and experiences. Providing a way for students to experience concepts, explore ideas and theories, and build perceptions allows for deeper understandings. Figure 3.1 illustrates how all of these inputs merge to form meanings of concepts.

Figure 3.1. Inputs to Developing Conceptual Understandings

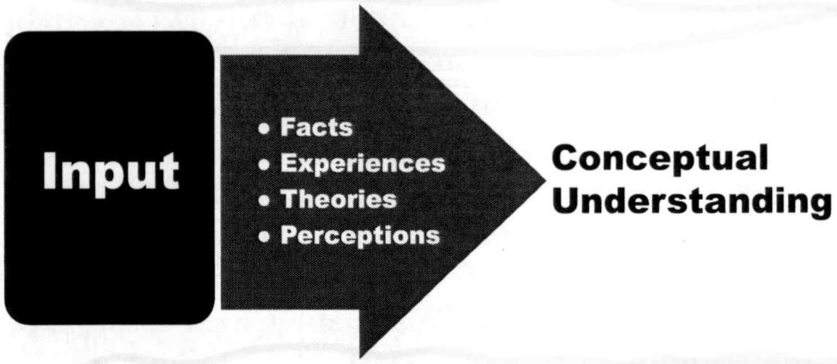

Input
- Facts
- Experiences
- Theories
- Perceptions

Conceptual Understanding

What Does Research Say about the Connection Between Teaching Concepts and Student Achievement?

Students whose teachers emphasize meaning perform *better* academically than peers whose teachers did not, and a focus on facts instead of reasoning can lead to *decreased* student achievement according to various studies.[3] Facts are important as they can help build the foundation for understanding concepts. The issue lies with focusing only on facts rather than on conceptual understanding. Hands-on and minds-on experiences are provided by teachers whose work results in *increased* student achievement because those experiences offer students linkages to bridge from concrete understanding to abstract thought.[4] Figure 3.2 provides findings from studies that support the impact of teaching for meaning on student achievement.

Figure 3.2. Teaching for Meaning and Student Achievement

Related Findings	Citation
◆ In a study of the link between teacher practices and student achievement, students whose teachers emphasized higher order thinking, rather than a focus on isolated facts, outperformed their counterparts.	Wenglinsky, 2000
◆ A study that examined instructional practices and achievement gaps in schools found that the more teachers used real-world problem solving the better the students performed on the National Assessment of Educational Progress (NAEP).	Wenglinsky, 2004
◆ A study examined the effects of a concept-oriented instructional strategy on understanding of text and found that third and fifth grade students receiving this type of instruction had better comprehension of text than did students receiving traditional instruction.	Guthrie et al., 1998
◆ A study of the achievement of third grade students found that teachers whose students achieved at the highest levels focused on teaching for meaning rather than a focus on memorization.	Stronge, Ward, Tucker, & Hindman, 2008

How Can a Teacher Use the Concept Attainment Teaching Model to Ensure that Students Make Meaningful Connections?

Students learn concepts in many ways, through both formal and informal means. In fact, schooling—that is, good schooling—ensures that students encounter learning concepts on an ongoing basis. One theorist described these as scientific concepts. Students also develop concepts as a result of everyday living—sometimes described as everyday concepts.[5] For example, a child learns about how plants grow in school and may even study the growth of carrots. In everyday life the child has carrots for dinner or for a snack. The study of carrots in school is systematic, while the interaction with carrots at home is not part of a systematic study of the carrot. It is a combination of the two types of concepts that leads to deeper understandings.

A kindergarten student will be exposed to many new concepts—hundreds if not thousands of concepts—between that first day of school and graduation day 13 years later. The first time the student encounters the term *noun*, the concept is new. Teachers use various ways to describe nouns to young children, such as "a naming thing" or a "person, place, or thing." In classrooms across the United States and elsewhere students are shown many examples of nouns to solidify their understanding of the concept. The understanding is then expanded to include the difference between a common noun and a proper noun, a noun's place in sentence structure, and so on. The important point is that educators teach new concepts to students every day. How teachers go about teaching them should be thoughtfully and carefully planned and implemented for best results.

Approaches to the Concept Attainment Model

Various approaches may be used to teach concepts, the concept attainment model of instruction is one prominent method. The concept attainment model of instruction "requires a student to figure out the attributes of a category that is already formed in another person's mind by comparing and contrasting examples that contain the characteristics of the concept with examples that do not."[6] A review of research in the early 1970s found 250 research studies that were conducted in the area of concept attainment.[7] It is still supported as a research-based model today.[8] There are, however, varying approaches to concept attainment including definition, structural comparisons, and examples/nonexamples.[9] Figure 3.3 provides a description of each approach.

Figure 3.3. Three Concept Attainment Strategies

Strategy	Description	Example
Definition	Teacher provides definition of concept and shows many examples	Teacher provides a definition of parallelogram and shows students many examples of parallelograms
Structural comparisons	Students explore similarities and differences between two concepts	Students research similarities and differences of parallelograms and other shapes
Examples/nonexamples	Teacher provides both positive and negative examples of a concept for student identification	Teacher provides examples of parallelograms and nonexamples of parallelograms eliciting from the students a definition of a parallelogram

This section focuses on the concept attainment model in which examples alone, or examples and nonexamples, are used to teach concepts. These strategies can be used to focus on specific concepts in which students must use inductive reasoning as they work with the examples.[10]

Research studies have examined the examples and nonexamples approach to concept attainment by studying:

♦ The effects of the order in which examples and nonexamples are presented;

♦ Whether examples and nonexamples should be presented in a rational or a random sequence; and

♦ Whether missed instances of the examples should be recycled to ensure student understanding.[11]

Regardless of the order in which examples are provided, studies show that the examples-only or the examples/nonexamples approach results in increased student understanding of the concept being studied.[12]

Implementing Concept Attainment

The *Concept Attainment Lesson Planning Template* in Figure 3.4 (page 44) can assist in planning a lesson using the concept attainment model and, thus, successful implementation in the classroom (a blank reproducible copy of the *Concept Attainment Lesson Planning Template* is found in Part II). The sample lesson focuses on the concepts of renewable and nonrenewable resources—common concepts studied in science. Steps 1 through 5 help teachers think through and carry out the lesson while Steps 6 through 8 are critical in successful implementation in the classroom, having students develop their own definitions of renewable and nonrenewable resources through examples of each. Depending on the concept being studied, teachers may show three- or two-dimensional examples. Figure 3.5 (page 44) provides an outline of the steps in the planning and implementation process.

Figure 3.4. Sample Completed Concept Attainment Lesson Planning Template

Concepts: Renewable and Nonrenewable Resources

Learning objectives:

1. To distinguish between renewable and nonrenewable resources

2. To describe the critical attributes of renewable and nonrenewable resources

3. To define concepts of renewable and nonrenewable resources

Definitions, Critical Attributes, and Examples of Concepts	
Concept 1: Renewable Resources Definition: Resources that can be naturally replaced or grown by people Critical Attributes: 1. Naturally occurring resources 2. Resources that can be replaced by humans	*Concept 2: Nonrenewable Resources* Definition: Resources that cannot be replaced once they are used up Critical Attributes: 1. Resources found in nature that cannot be replaced 2. Resources that cannot be grown by humans
Examples: trees fish oranges chickens solar energy	*Examples:* coal gasoline oil gold oceans

Figure 3.5. Concept Attainment Model Planning and Implementation Process

Lesson Planning

Step 1: Decide what concept students are to learn. This decision is influenced by national and state standards, as well as school district curricula.

Step 2: Develop learning goals for the lesson.

Step 3: Develop a clear definition of the concepts and the critical attributes of each.

Step 4: Choose examples that clearly demonstrate the concept(s).

Step 5: Present clear examples first, moving toward more difficult examples.

Lesson Implementation

Step 6: Have students hypothesize about the critical attributes of the concept(s).

Step 7: Have students test hypotheses with subsequent examples.

Step 8: Work with students to develop a definition of the concept(s).

By Using Questioning as an Instructional Strategy

Why Should Teachers Use Questioning in Instruction?

The short answer is because questioning engages learners in the instructional process and provides the teacher with valuable information about student learning. Effective questioning is an often ignored, but, nonetheless, essential component of teaching. A teacher may ask 300 to 400 questions a day,[13] but if the questions are not aligned with the desired learning outcomes, then what is the point? Questions need to be strategically planned to involve learners and help them connect important concepts while providing the teacher with needed information. For effective teachers, questioning fulfills a variety of needs such as:

- ◆ Preassessment,
- ◆ Feedback on instruction,
- ◆ Insights on students' misconceptions,
- ◆ Assessment, and
- ◆ A means to provoke inquiry.

> **Four Characteristics of Effective Questioning**
>
> 1. Promote one or more instructional purposes,
> 2. Focus on important content,
> 3. Facilitate thinking at a stipulated cognitive level, and
> 4. Communicate clearly what is being asked.[14]

Effective teachers use various formats to ask questions and engage their students, but they are not the only sources of questions. Student questioning is encouraged as students are taught how to formulate inquiries for their teachers and peers in addition to providing responses. (See sidebar for four characteristics of effective questioning.)

What Does Research Say About the Connection Between Questioning and Student Achievement?

Teachers possess varying abilities when it comes to questioning. The best teachers use questioning as a means to engage students' minds to help them construct knowledge, resulting in increased student learning. Figure 3.6 (page 46) summarizes selected research findings related to questioning and student achievement.

Figure 3.6. Questioning and Student Achievement

Related Findings	Citation
◆ Effective teachers asked more questions at the application and above-classification levels, whereas less effective teachers asked more comprehension-level questions; there was no difference in the number of recall (knowledge) questions asked.	Stronge, Tucker, & Ward, 2003
◆ Researchers found that young students of teachers adept at questioning tend to have better language development and analytical thinking skills than peers with teachers who are not as well versed in using questioning techniques.	Martin, Sexton, & Gerlovich, 2004
◆ After controlling for prior achievement, researchers found that more effective teachers whose students achieved at high levels asked seven times as many higher-level questions as teachers whose students underperformed on state standardized assessments.	Stronge, Ward, Tucker, & Hindman, 2008
◆ First through fifth grade students in high-poverty schools whose teachers employed higher-level questions achieved greater growth in reading.	Taylor, Pearson, Peterson, & Rodriguez, 2003

What Should Teachers Consider When Developing and Implementing Questioning in the Classroom?

Debunking Some Myths About Questioning

Effective use of questioning strategies is a means to reduce the time a teacher spends talking and increase student learning and participation. However, myths about questions persist in the minds of teachers. One author presents nine questioning myths related to class discussions; they are summarized in Figure 3.7.[15] The summary is followed by a discussion refuting the myths. The author suggests that teachers rely more on intuition when it comes to questioning as opposed to making systematic decisions about what and how they will question. For example, questions requiring students to apply prior knowledge to new situations generate engagement and new learning. Furthermore, student-to-student interaction in the questioning process is valuable as students query one another. Also, appropriately challenging questions enhance student engagement and learning.

Figure 3.7. Myths and Realities about Questioning in the Classroom

Myth	Reality
Questioning does not require planning.	Planning key questions to guide a lesson provides structure and a point to return if the discussion becomes divergent; it also increases student engagement and understanding.
More questions equal more student learning.	For lower-cognitive questions requiring recall of information, many fast-paced questions may be appropriate; however, particularly with high-cognitive questions, quality is better than quantity as students need time to analyze and formulate responses.
Every question is a good question.	Questions that confuse students, ask for yes/no responses, are vague, or use unfamiliar vocabulary actually decrease participation.
Higher-level questions are better than lower-level questions.	Asking questions within a range of levels is necessary as students build their knowledge and skills. Although simple recalling of facts is rarely the final goal, it often is a step for laying the foundation for higher-level inquiry.
High-level questions equal high-level responses.	Often what the teacher intends to ask is not aligned with what students perceive is asked. Teachers need to share with students expectations of how to respond to higher-level questions so students are aware of key words that can cue them to the type of question being asked.
Lower-level questions always come before higher-level questions.	Depending on the desired outcome, a teacher may want to start with a higher-level cognitive question to encourage students to form opinions, then use lower-level questioning to get students to support their positions with facts. Whether one is working up or working down, the cognitive challenge of the question needs to be aligned with the intended learning outcome.
Students have enough wait time.	Often teachers do not wait as long as they think they do for student responses. Three to five seconds is recommended.[16]
Calling on volunteers is better.	When dealing with sensitive issues, a teacher may prefer calling on volunteers. In general, however, both students who volunteer and those who do not need to be involved in the class discussion.
Teachers encourage student-generated questions.	As students grow older, they tend to ask fewer information-seeking questions or probing questions.

Attending to the Cognitive Level of Questions

Bloom's *Taxonomy for Cognitive Objectives*, which many teachers learned about in education courses and professional development settings, was developed about 50 years ago through the collaborative efforts of scholars. Most likely, Bloom's taxonomy was and is used in helping preservice teachers to write behavioral, measurable objectives. However, Bloom's taxonomy can also be used to develop and implement questions at the range of cognitive levels (see sidebar). Bloom's taxonomy includes six levels: knowledge, comprehension, application, analysis, synthesis and evaluation. Questions on eminent domain provide an example of how to classify questions, which is explained in Figure 3.8.

Figure 3.8. Difference in Levels of Questions

Question	Bloom's Taxonomy Level	Rationale
What is the power of eminent domain?	Comprehension	The response indicates that students understand the concept of eminent domain.
How does the power of eminent domain impact people in your town who live in the area of the proposed arena?	Analysis	The response requires the students to have an understanding of eminent domain, apply this understanding to situation, and then to *analyze* the situation for the impact of eminent domain.

Cognitive Levels of Questions

Questions may be classified in a variety of ways, Bloom's taxonomy[17] (i.e., knowledge, comprehension, application, analysis, synthesis, and evaluation) is commonly used and is discussed in a later section of this chapter. In effective teacher research (see for example Stronge & Tucker, 2002), the taxonomy is divided into low, intermediate, and high cognitive levels.

♦ *Low Level:* recall/knowledge

♦ *Intermediate Level:* comprehension

♦ *High Level:* application, analysis, synthesis, evaluation

Applying Bloom's, or any cognitive taxonomy framework, to questioning is one way to consider whether questions are appropriately targeted for the type of knowledge and the cognitive challenge desired.

Waiting for Students to Think About Questions and Formulate a Response

Two seconds can make a great deal of difference in student response to questions. One researcher analyzed hundreds of teacher audiotapes and found that teachers often asked a question, then waited about a second before seeking a response; however, when the silence extended to three seconds or more, there were numerous positive benefits.[20] She called this silence "wait time." There are two kinds of wait time: Wait Time 1 is the silence right after the question is posed and Wait Time 2 is the pause after the student responds before the next speaker (usually the teacher) talks. This time allows students and teachers to process information and think about what has been said, seen, and done before tendering a response. Based on the research, some of the positive benefits of wait time include:

♦ More students volunteer to respond, including those who do not often participate when there is less wait time.[21]

♦ Responses are detailed, reflective, and accurate.

♦ Student-initiated questions and responses increase.

♦ Student-to-student interaction increases.[22]

♦ Student achievement improves.

♦ Scores on academic achievement tests increase.[23]

♦ Teachers tend to ask fewer questions, but the questions they do ask are of higher quality.

♦ Higher expectations for students are communicated.

♦ Teachers ask questions that require more complex information processing and higher-level thinking.[24]

> **Bloom's Taxonomy Revised**
>
> In 2001, scholars introduced *The Taxonomy of Educational Objectives*, a revised taxonomy that is two-dimensional. This taxonomy "is a scheme for classifying educational goals, objectives, and most recently, standards;"[18] yet just as the original Bloom's taxonomy works well for question classification, so does this one. This updated version includes *both* a cognitive process dimension and knowledge dimension. Key differences between the original and revised taxonomies are: (1) levels are expressed as verbs such as *remember* instead of *knowledge*, (2) some of the terms have changed, (3) the last two cognitive process levels have been switched with *evaluate* preceding *create*—what was called *synthesis* in the original taxonomy.[19] Another key difference is the knowledge dimension, which demonstrates student thinking from concrete to abstract.

Figure 3.9 summarizes what works and what does not work for classroom questioning. Oftentimes, when teachers are planning lessons, they neglect to plan questions, resulting in questions that may not be the best use of class time. Not that all questions need be planned, but a lack of planning may lead to poorly phrased, random questions that add little to the instructional process. A few well-constructed questions committed to paper or electronic media can ensure that questions related to instructional goals are asked at an appropriate time, at the intended level, and use vocabulary the students will understand. There is quite a difference between asking a student "What is the power of eminent domain?" versus "How does the power of eminent domain impact people in your town who live in the area of the proposed arena?" A teacher purposefully may ask the first question—a low-level one (see sidebar page 48)—to ensure that students remember what eminent domain means, but then follows up with a higher-level question that demands more as students apply the power to a specific situation. By waiting after the question is asked, teachers allow students time to organize their thoughts before articulating their responses. As noted earlier, this time delay following a question often results in higher levels of student involvement and higher quality responses.[25]

Figure 3.9. What Works and What Doesn't Work in Questioning

What Works?	What Doesn't Work?
☑ Planning questions ☑ Purposeful questioning ☑ Questions that vary by level ☑ Wait time	☒ Extemporaneous questions ☒ Lack of order to the questions ☒ Trivial questions ☒ Vague questions

How Can Teachers Evaluate Their Own Questioning Practices?

An effective teacher is a reflective practitioner. It can be difficult, however, if not impossible, to remember all the questions asked and how students responded in order to reflect specifically on one's questioning practices. The template, *Teacher Questioning Practices Record,* provided in Figure 3.10, enables a teacher to examine his or her own questioning practices (a blank reproducible copy of the *Teacher Questioning Practices Record* is available in Part II). Use of the form involves either a colleague or administrator observing a class or videotaping a lesson that the teacher can analyze for questioning.

Collecting Data

The *Teacher Questioning Practices Record* (Figure 3.10) collects several pieces of information related to teachers' questioning practices. First, the observer writes each question that was asked and classifies it according to a taxonomy that incorporates Bloom's taxonomy within a three-level system.[26] The lowest cognitive level is called "recall," the mid-level containing understanding, applying, and analyzing questions is termed "use," and "create" is the high-cognitive level where students must extend their learning. The wait time, the seconds between when the question is posed and when the first response is sought, is noted. Finally, the observer indicates who responds to the question: Is it a volunteer or a nonvolunteer? Is the student male or female? After the lesson concludes, the observer totals the number of questions by type, identifies the mode for wait time, and summarizes the information about those who answered questions. The teacher and the observer, if one is used, examine the data and begin the reflective process.

The completed template provides a glimpse into a second grade reading teacher's questioning practices. She read a book on Australia to her students and a colleague wrote down all the questions she asked.

Figure 3.10. Teacher Questioning Practices Record

Teacher Questioning Practices Record   Sheet 1 of 1

Teacher's Name 2nd Grade Teacher   Date February 12   Start Time 9:00 a.m. End Time 9:25 a.m.

Directions: Record each teacher-posed question—including follow up probes and cues—in the first column. Next, classify the question. In the next column, indicate the approximate amount of wait time in seconds. Finally, record who responds to the question by using either an "M" for male or "F" for female. Should the teacher call on multiple responders for a question, note a number by each letter to show the order.

Question	Recall	Use	Create	Wait Time (seconds)	Responder — Volunteer	Responder — Nonvolunteer
What did I see in the jungle?	✓			1	X	
What do you know about kangaroos?	✓			1		X
What types of colors might kangaroos be?	✓			1	X	
What is Australia surrounded by?	✓			1	X	
Do you think you could put a kangaroo in a car and drive from Australia to New Jersey?		✓		3		X
Could you fly to Australia?		✓		1	X	
What did we hear about wallabies?	✓			1		X
What animal does it look like?		✓		2		X
What is a title page?	✓			1	X	
What did we learn about kangaroos?	✓			1	X	
Directions: Total the information for each column in this row. If multiple sheets were used, write the grand total for each column on the first page and circle those numbers.	Total # 7	Total # 3	Total # 0	Mode 1	# Males 2 / # Females 4	# Males 2 / # Females 2

* Walsh and Sattes' Taxonomy: **Recall** indicates the student is remembering information that was taught; **Use** refers to the student implementing the information taught; and **Create** addresses times when the student must go beyond what was taught to formulate a response.

Reflecting on the Data

In reflecting on the data, teachers may consider questions such as:

♦ What patterns are evident in the questioning data?

♦ How does the data align with what the teacher anticipated?

♦ What area is a likely place to target for enhancement of professional practice?

♦ How will I begin to improve?

♦ What resources do I need?

The data also may lead teachers to want more information before deciding if and how to proceed. The teacher may want to see if there is a distribution pattern in who is called upon to respond by using a seating chart in which an observer notes who and how often a student answers a question or initiates a question. Other possible next steps include:

♦ Analyzing the type of feedback provided to the student.

♦ Raising the level of student responses to questions.

♦ Teaching students how to ask questions.

The second grade teacher notices in the data that she asked questions mainly at the recall or comprehension levels, with few at the use level, and none at the create level. She most frequently waited only one second for students to respond and she called on volunteers and nonvolunteers about equally. The data also show that she called equally on boys and girls. The teacher may need to consider changing her questioning to address higher cognitive levels and to increase wait time based on her reflection on the classroom data.

By Developing Inquiring Minds

What is Inquiry-Based Instruction and Why Should Teachers Use It?

A quick tour through the extant research and practitioner literature reveals that *hands-on learning* and *inquiry* mean different things to different people, yet these terms often get used interchangeably. A common denominator of both types of learning is that students are actively involved. The learning approaches work in a variety of settings and content areas. Teachers invite students to engage in constructing knowledge as they take into account students' prior knowledge.[27]

Science, music, art, physical education, and vocational education classes have long benefited from the use of inquiry and hands-on learning experiences. Yet, the nudge to actively involve students in their learning and the rise of *hands-on learning* and *inquiry* began about 25 years ago. The 1983 release of *A Nation At-Risk* followed by the 1994 *Goals 2000 Act* signaled a paradigm shift from the behaviorist (i.e., Skinnerian) approach of instructing students towards a more interactive inquiry approach (i.e., Socratic).[28] This shift occurred in part as a result of the needs of the workforce where critical thinking, lifelong learning, and an ability to adapt to new job demands are essential. In the United States in the early 1900s, 95% of jobs were relatively low-skilled, but by the start of the 21st century the percentage had decreased to 10%.[29] At the center of this paradigm shift is the duel between the "tell me" mode of instruction and the "involve me" mode of facilitating learning (Figure 3.11).

Figure 3.11. Role of the Teacher between the "Tell Me" and "Involve Me" Modes of Learning[30]

Factor	Tell Me	Involve Me
Communication	Teacher controls the communication.	Leader facilitates communication using ground rules. Students initiate communication.
Conflict management	Teacher manages conflicts.	Leader teaches students how to handle their own conflicts.
Problem solving	Teacher solves the problems.	Leader teaches the model for solving problems. Leader ensures that students have access to resources to solve problems. Students take responsibility for identifying and solving problems they encounter.
Feedback	Teacher provides feedback.	Leader helps students learn how to provide and seek feedback effectively. Leader and students give feedback to each other and critique their own performances jointly through self-critique.

Hands-on activities naturally lend themselves to being interdisciplinary. Consider the integration of technology education and mathematics at the secondary level in an activity to design a staircase. Students use mathematical formulas and functions (e.g., slope, Pythagorean theorem) to design a new stairway. By connecting to standards in another subject area, "students will begin to see the connections of linchpins that connect different fields of learning."[31]

A teacher's role in inquiry learning does need to change, depending on the subject, level of complexity, and the intended practical applications of the learning. For instance, instead of being "the Master and Commander of Learning," the teacher may become more of a facilitator of learning. Hands-on/minds-on inquiry is a way to empower students to identify problems, analyze information, and formulate conclusions. At the same time, the teacher moves into a position of facilitating students' learning as opposed to instructing them on the important details to memorize. Thus, the teacher provides a forum for interactive and responsive education.

What Does Research Say About the Connection Between an Inquiry-Based Approach and Student Learning?

Educators and researchers know that activities that increase student achievement are those that encourage collaboration, engage students with hands-on learning, and individual instruction.[32] Figure 3.12 provides a summary of selected research findings related to elements of inquiry-based instruction and student achievement.

How Does a Teacher Adapt an Activity to Enhance Inquiry-Based Learning?

Important Considerations

Inquiry-based learning is a means to unite real world and classroom experiences. Teachers act as facilitators providing support for content learning, using multiple forms of assessment, and modeling behaviors and skills that students will need to be successful. These teachers:

♦ Watch for cues from students so they know when to nudge or ask a probing question,

♦ Develop students' collaboration skills so students can work effectively with others,

♦ Guide students so students control their topic investigations, while the teacher still effectively manages the classroom, and

♦ Constructively use mistakes to help students refine their thinking.

Figure 3.12. Inquiry-Based Instruction and Student Achievement

Related Findings	Citation
◆ Students whose teachers used hands-on learning outperformed their peers by 70% of a grade level in math and 40% of a grade level in science.	Wenglinsky, 2000
◆ A study of 8,000 middle school students in Detroit Public Schools found that student achievement significantly increased over a span of three years for each year students participated in a revised science curriculum that emphasized inquiry-based instruction in the program.	Marx et al., 2004
◆ In a study of high school mathematics achievement, researchers found that when teachers reported using reform-oriented practices that included an inquiry-based approach, their students who were enrolled in integrated mathematics courses performed better on the Stanford 9 Achievement Test than did students whose teachers used reform practices within traditional mathematics courses. Therefore, the use of inquiry-based instruction must be coupled with a curriculum that supports inquiry-based instruction.	McCaffrey et al., 2001
◆ A study of the use of inquiry-based instruction in science with English Language Learners found positive effects in achievement in science, reading, writing, and mathematics. The longer the students were in the inquiry-based instructional program the greater their scores on the Stanford 9 Achievement Test for science, reading, and mathematics, and on a locally developed and administered writing prompt.	Amaral, Garrison, & Klentschy, 2002

Setting Up an "Inquiry Environment"

For students, inquiry-learning situations are filled with both benefits and challenges. Certainly, a well-constructed inquiry lesson will provide the student with deeper understanding of the content and skill development. However, years of school experience often drills into students that teachers ask questions and students answer them with responses the teacher says are correct or incorrect. Often students initially are uncomfortable with the teacher as a coach and the student as a leader, so building gradually is important. In inquiry, students are actively involved—engaged in the process to plan and execute investigations on a topic. Students determine the question to be addressed, research the problem, propose reasonable explanations for addressing the question, often ask additional questions, and critique their process.

Matching the Inquiry Task to the Learner's Needs

The use of inquiry is strengthened when teachers recognize that there are different levels of inquiry and match students to the appropriate level, thus, creating an attainable cognitive challenge. Additionally, teachers can "stretch" students to build their capacities and as students demonstrate competence a teacher may introduce a task aimed at a different level of inquiry. For inquiry to work, students need effective social and communication skills, which can be developed throughout the school year. For example, teachers can model for students how to engage in a cycle of "do, talk, reflect, and write" so students have an opportunity to develop their process skills and refine their thinking.

Adapting an Activity for Inquiry-Based Instruction

One way for teachers to get more out of inquiry is to examine currently developed activities that address the curriculum that the teacher likes to teach and to which students respond favorably. The *Inquiry-Based Lesson Adaptation Template* (a completed sample of which appears in Figure 3.13) is an example of how a lesson was adapted to include inquiry (a blank reproducible copy of the *Inquiry-Based Lesson Adaptation Template* is available in Part II). A middle school social studies teacher enjoys teaching about muckrakers and the students usually enjoy the topic and the lessons that the teacher presents. The teacher, however, wants to move this topic to a higher cognitive level—one that includes inquiry.

In the muckraker activity, the teacher traditionally told the students the day before that they were going to be rewarded for something they had done. The teacher pulled the "celery strings" from a bunch of celery and added them to the brownie mix prior to baking. The next day, students received their brownie squares. Typically, several students notice the celery immediately and ask the teacher who feigns being shocked. This leads to a discussion of the assigned reading from the night before on muckrakers and what they found. The teacher reveals that celery had been added to the brownies and they were safe to eat or students could trade them in for brownies without celery strings. This activity makes *muckraker's* memorable as a term, but is the lowest level of inquiry as students just confirm what the teacher has set up.

To increase the inquiry level, the teacher could question students about what they found, their concerns, and what they want to do about it. This increases the inquiry level just slightly as the conclusions are drawn by the students as opposed to predetermined by the teacher. If students are already comfortable with voicing conclusions, the teacher could take another route. Feed the brownies to the students, go through the findings of the celery strings, disclose to the students that yes, the teacher had indeed added them, but ask student to consider what they would do if they had purchased the brownies from a store. Students' thoughts and questions could be channeled into what governments do to protect consumers and the historical background.

The template provided is used to help a teacher think through an activity to determine if going up an inquiry level is worthwhile. The template in Figure 3.13 has been filled in with a teacher's thought process as she reflected on how to get more out of the inquiry activity. She answered the questions about the potential inquiry expansion of having students consider what they would do if they had bought the brownie. If the purpose of the activity had been a "quick" demonstration, it may not make sense to enhance the activity. However, most hands-on activities can be revised by expanding the students' role.

Figure 3.13. Sample Completed Inquiry-Based Lesson Adaptation Template

Adapting an Activity to Inquiry-Based Learning

Activity's Name: Muckrakers to the Rescue

Resources to Use: Teacher-developed activity

Focus: Role of muckrakers in highlighting public safety issues

Justifying the Inquiry: What are learning outcomes related to the inquiry?

♦ Understanding of who muckrakers were and what they did

♦ Knowledge of the Pure Food and Drug Act of 1906 and related Meat Packing Act of 1906

♦ Application to students' lives 100 years later

Building up to the Inquiry: What activities and learning experiences have students had or will have had to prepare them for the inquiry?

♦ Theodore Roosevelt's administration

♦ Researching on the Internet—verifying information and checking facts

♦ Excerpts from Upton Sinclair's *The Jungle* discussion the previous day

♦ Interaction of federal, state, and local governments

Thinking Through the Inquiry: What are the items and issues related to this topic?

♦ *Social Studies topics:* review of the Spanish American War (soldiers ate embalmed meat)

♦ *Interdisciplinary connections:* English/Language Arts with the analysis of political cartoons

Identifying Likely Supports Tools: What resources will I need to support the inquiry? What resources will likely be needed by students?

♦ Brownie Mix and celery

♦ Copies of the history of the Pure Food and Drugs Act

(Figure continues on next page.)

- ◆ Access to the Internet

- ◆ Meeting with the cafeteria manager so they can ask questions about health inspections

Identifying Potential Barriers: What barriers may exist in completing the inquiry lesson?

- ◆ Checked on food allergies; student discomfort with the fact that there is "no one right response"

- ◆ Time

Completing the Inquiry: How will students know that they've arrived at a stopping point? How will I provide feedback on the students' inquiry process?

1. When they have developed a course of action that they would take (e.g., complaint letter to the bakery, notification to the health department)

2. Querying students on their reasons for why action or no action is justified, encourage students to consider what life would be like without the FDA of 1906

Considering the Potential Investment: How long will the inquiry take? Is it worth it?

- ◆ Time: 2-3 days

- ◆ Yes, students usually remember the brownies and the muckrakers, but the outcomes of the muckraker's actions are often lost after the unit test

Reflecting on the Inquiry-Based Learning Experience: What questions do I still have?

Fill in after the activity.

By Increasing Student Engagement Through Challenging Instruction

What Is Involved in Challenging Instruction and Why Is It Important?

Student engagement, simply put, is students appropriately participating in instruction. High levels of student engagement are associated with student success[33] and greater enjoyment of class.[34] So what constitutes challenging instruction? Challenging instruction assumes many forms from discussion to song writing, with common elements of high cognitive challenge, high expectations, and relevance to students' lives.

High Cognitive Challenge

Effective teachers know when a student earning a B on an assignment is good and when it is just "getting by." Some students are disengaged because what they are asked to do may be appropriate for most of the class, but not for them. Adjusting the level of challenge within an assignment is one way of meeting different student needs.

High Expectations

Reaching high expectations is part conveying to students belief in their abilities and the teacher's ability to offer a healthy dose of support. Articles and resources abound about how to promote high expectations and the impact of them. One program, Teacher Expectations and Student Achievement (TESA), is being used to support teachers in fostering teacher–student connections to promote student engagement in learning. Teachers focus on how they interact with students when they are encouraging participation, giving feedback, and showing regard (e.g., building rapport, managing misbehavior).[7] TESA training sensitizes teachers to the expectations they have for students and their behaviors towards students which convey those expectations.

Teachers use a variety of tools, including scaffolding experiences, to provide students with support to be successful with challenging instruction. As students experience success, the teacher provides opportunities to use existing skills and knowledge as well as attain new competencies.[8] By having reasonable expectations for students' growth, teachers can plan carefully linked experiences to provide the foundation for students to meet high expectations.[9] Throughout these experiences, the teacher consistently reinforces the importance of doing one's best.

High Relevance

Being cognitively invested in a task is not enough to optimize student engagement; students need to be invested emotionally in their work. Plenty of students can go through the exercise of graphing data, writing a persuasive essay, and reading about local history. Yet, when a student applies all these academic tasks to an issue of interest, then the learning really takes off. Students marshal their resources and extend themselves to get additional skills and knowledge to address a challenge.

What Does the Research Say About Student Engagement and Student Learning?

High levels of student engagement are associated with student success,[36] greater enjoyment of class,[37] and challenging instruction in which teachers match task complexities and individual skills.[38] When an

---

Making Good on Delivering Challenging Instruction

To deliver challenging instruction, teachers need to:[35]

♦ Demonstrate their professional expertise by:

- Adapting lessons to differentiate the challenge level for different learners

- Selecting and using a variety of instructional strategies

- Setting appropriate cognitive goals and challenges for students

♦ Involve students by:

- Encouraging students to ask questions

- Holding students accountable for learning and understanding

- Providing opportunities for students to use and expand their skills

- Appealing to students' desires to enjoy what they are doing

---

appropriate match occurs, students are motivated and engaged, but when the task is not aligned to student skill levels then engagement and motivation decrease.[39] Figure 3.14 provides a sample of research findings related to student engagement and student achievement.

Figure 3.14. Student Engagement and Student Achievement

Related Findings	Citation
◆ When elementary and middle school students reported high levels of engagement, they were 44 to 75% more likely to perform better on academic and behavioral indicators. Additionally, when elementary school students reported high levels of support from their teachers, they were 89% more likely to feel engaged.	Klem & Connell, 2004
◆ A longitudinal study of high school students found that students were more engaged when tasks required highly developed skills, were challenging, and were relevant to their lives. They also reported higher levels of self-esteem when they were engaged in learning.	Shernoff, Csikszentmihalyi, Schneider, & Shernoff, 2003
◆ A study which examined the relationship between teacher instructional practices and student achievement in reading found that high engagement in the classroom was positively associated with students' reading comprehension.	Taylor, Pearson, Peterson, & Rodriguez, 2003

How Can a Teacher Determine if Students Are Engaged?

Student engagement is an issue for both classroom management and instructional delivery. In terms of classroom management, the focus is on individual student's behavior. Although the instructional delivery component emphasizes what is occurring in the classroom, in essence it is the context for the behaviors that occur. The *Student Engagement Record Template* in Figure 3.15 can be used to collect data on both facets of student engagement as one does influence the other (a blank reproducible copy of the *Student Engagement Record* is available in Part II).

Classroom Management Facet

Engaging instruction can be a means to manage the classroom. Students who are engaged in the lesson or productively with their peers are interacting in the classroom in a positive manner. There are some teachers whose classroom management skills are not as smooth as other colleagues, but their high-interest lessons motivate students to become involved leaving little room for misbehavior. Yet, no one is engaged 100% of the time. Some students who are not engaged may only affect their own learning as they read, think about other topics, or doodle. Other disengaged students may actively

Figure 3.15. Student Engagement Record Template

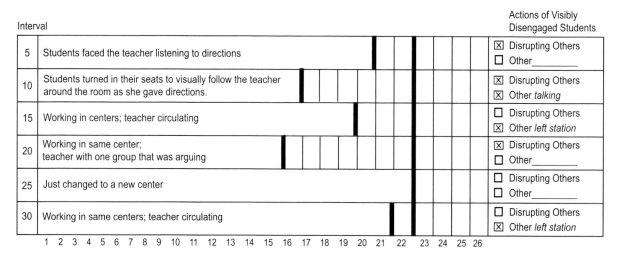

disrupt the learning of others by disturbing peers and necessitating the teacher to stop instruction to address the behavior.

The last column of the *Student Engagement Record* provides a place for an observer to note the misbehavior of disengaged students. A teacher likely will recall redirecting a student or addressing a behavior issue if the student's actions disrupted others, but the teacher may not have been aware of a student who is simply not attending to the lesson. A visibly disengaged student is someone who does not appear to be doing what the rest of the class is doing. For example, if the class is taking notes, this person is not writing. The possibility does exist that the individual does not need to take notes (e.g., the notes are provided because of a fine motor disability). However in this example, the student probably would not be misbehaving; rather, the observer would check "other" and indicate what the student was doing.

Instructional Delivery Facet

Some classrooms buzz with students moving around the room and talking about a content-related topic whereas others have quieter instructional activities occurring. In both situations, learning is occurring. Teachers select effective instructional strategies and resources to teach the subject knowledge and skills to students. Often, engaging instruction involves relating the lesson to students' lives and prior knowledge, creating motivating experiences, and having high expectations for students. In turn, the students choose to participate. The motivation for each student likely is different whether it is an internal motivation such as desire to know more or an external motivation such as getting a good grade.

The *Student Engagement Record* provides a line next to each 5-minute interval in which an observer indicates how many students are engaged and what the class was doing when the observation was made. For example in a 45-minute observation, one likely will see peaks and valleys reflecting

> *Tacit Knowledge*—information that one knows from experience.

increasing and decreasing levels of engagement. Most educators' tacit knowledge tells them to expect decreased engagement during transitions; hence effective teachers establish routines so that the momentum of instruction is not lost.

Considerations for Using the Form

The observation provides a running record of what occurred in the classroom. It links the actions of engaged and disengaged students with those of the teacher. Review the data to determine if there is a pattern to when students are not engaged. Then reflect on what can be done to increase engagement. Remember that 100% engagement 100% of the time is unrealistic, but consistently high levels of engagement is a realistic goal.

Case in Point

One teacher who used this form noted that if her directions ran long that her students appeared disengaged, by reviewing the observations on the form she saw that sometimes she spent 10 minutes explaining how to do an activity before letting students start. The teacher was not as surprised by the students' reaction as she was that it took her so long to give directions. This teacher worked on other ways to give directions such as providing a quick overview of the activity with bulleted points so students had enough information to get started and execute the activity.

Summary

In this chapter, we provided four ways to enhance the instructional process to increase student motivation to learning and, in the end, to increase student learning. These four ways do not necessarily encompass the *most* effective ways of teaching but they are indeed supported by research as having a positive impact on student achievement. The key is not to use one strategy over another all of the time, but to use the appropriate instructional strategy at the appropriate time for effective teaching of the specific curriculum and with the specific students. Therefore, a teacher needs to know which strategies work best! Some of these strategies include planning and delivering instruction that:

♦ Emphasizes conceptual understanding rather than a focus on memorization of disjointed facts;

♦ Uses questioning to engage and assess student learning during the instructional process;

♦ Develops inquiry minds by structuring instruction to allow for minds-on and hands-on learning; and

♦ Increases student engagement through instruction that is challenging and meaningful.

Notes

1   See, for example, Nye, Konstantopoulos, & Hedges, 2004; Wright, Horn, & Sanders, 1997.

2   Ornstein & Hunkins, 2004.

3   Mason, Schroeter, Combs, & Washington, 1992; Molnar, Smith, Zahorik, Palmer, Halbach, & Ehrle, 1999; National Research Council, 1999; Wenglinsky, 2004.

4   Wenglinsky, 2000; Wenglinsky, 2002.

5   Van der Veer, 1998.

6   Joyce & Weil, 2004, p. 62.

7   Clark, 1971.

8   Joyce, & Weil, 2004; Merrill & Tennyson, 1977.

9   McEachron, 2001.

10   Joyce & Weil, 2004.

11   Ford & McKinney, 1986; Hunnicut, & Larkins, 1985; Osmond & Jansson, 1987.

12   Joyce & Weil, 2004.

13   Brualdi, 1998.

14   Walsh & Sattes, 2005.

15   Wilen, 2001.

16   Rowe, 1972.

17   Bloom, Englehart, Furst, Hill, & Karthwohl, 1956.

18   Krathwohl, 2002.

19   Walsh & Sattes, 2005.

20   Rowe, 1972.

21   Cotton, 2001.

22   Cotton, 2001.

23   Stahl, 1994.

24   Stahl, 1994.

25   Good & Brophy, 1997.

26   Walsh & Sattes, 2005.

27   Covino & Iwanicki, 1996.

28   Sit, 2001.

29   Darling-Hammond, 2008.

30   Sit, 2001.

31   Merrill & Comerford, 2004.

32   Educational Research Services, 2000.

33   Brewster & Fager, 2000.

34 Bohn, Roehrig, & Pressley, 2004.

35 Committee on Increasing High School Students' Engagement and Motivation to Learn, 2004.

36 Brewster & Fager, 2000.

37 Bohn, Roehrig, & Pressley, 2004.

38 Csikszenthmilhalyi, Rathunde, & Whalen, 1993.

39 Csikszenthmilhalyi, Rathunde, & Whalen, 1993.

4

How Do Teachers Develop Assessments and Use Assessment Data to Improve Student Learning?

Assessment is a topic of high interest in today's accountability era. Students take tests at the classroom, school district, and state level. Their progress is monitored through the use of ongoing, incremental assessments designed to measure growth. What is most important in the discussion of assessment is *how* assessments are used. To move student learning forward, two types of assessment are necessary.[1] The first is assessment *of* learning, which involves making a summary judgment about student learning and is fairly well established in classrooms around the country. The second is assessment *for* learning, which involves using assessment information to make instructional decisions, which is gaining ground as one of the most effective ways that a teacher can impact student academic progress.[2]

The assessment *of* student learning is usually a known test based on known standards so teachers design instruction and assessments to address those known entities. Assessment *for* student learning includes activities that contribute to and inform the learning process. The bridge constructed by good teachers may simply be called alignment. When the bridge does not exist, then it "can cause numerous difficulties. For example, if instruction is not aligned with assessment then even the highest quality instruction likely will not lead to high student performance on assessments."[3] When teachers align the cognitive process and the knowledge level needed for success of external assessments, they can communicate goals to students and have a guide for the assessments they develop and use in their classrooms. In this process, teachers become increasingly assessment literate meaning they interpret test data (i.e., assessment *of* student learning) and develop action plans to improve student learning (i.e., assessment *for* student learning).[4]

This chapter focuses on both assessment *of* and *for* student learning. The question at the beginning of the chapter begs an answer: How does a teacher develop assessments and use assessment data to improve student learning? There are four distinct ways:

- By developing assessments that align with learning objectives

- By creating rubrics that communicate expectations to students

- By providing feedback to students that moves their learning forward

- By using assessment data to set student achievement goals

By Developing Assessments That Align with Learning Objectives

Why Should Teachers Develop Assessments That Align with Learning Objectives?

Types of Validity

Construct validity—Can we infer a student's ability in an area such as historical analysis or mathematics from the assessment?

Content validity—Does the end-of-unit assessment adequately sample the instructional objectives for the students?

Predictive validity—Can the end-of-unit assessment predict performance on a future assessment?

Consequential validity—What are the consequences of using this particular end-of-unit assessment for making a summative decision regarding student learning and are those consequences appropriate?

Regardless of specific uses of assessment information, the decisions based on this information are only as valid (i.e., appropriate) and reliable (i.e., consistent) as the assessments that are administered. There are several types of validity that need to be considered (see sidebar). For example, if a mathematics teacher has students complete exit cards before they leave class about the day's lesson on cross-multiplying fractions and the problems on the exit cards require students to reduce fractions, the information from the exit cards will be of limited use in knowing whether students grasp cross-multiplication. This is an example of a validity issue. To ensure sound validity, however, the assessment must be aligned with the curriculum and instruction.

What Does Research Say About the Connection Between Aligned Assessments and Student Learning?

Alignment of assessments indicates that the assessments are aligned both to the curriculum (i.e. state or national standards) and to classroom instruction. For students to learn, they need to be exposed to the right content, at the right cognitive level, and in the right way! Studies which have examined the content that teachers actually teach, and may or may not assess have found that content coverage from classroom to classroom varies significantly.[5] If the instructional content is not aligned, then it is logical to assume that assessments are not aligned with the content that students should be learning. Figure 4.1 provides findings from studies that support the impact of teaching for meaning on student achievement.

Figure 4.1. Aligned Assessments and Student Learning

Related Findings	Citation
♦ A study that examined teacher-made tests found that teachers emphasized knowledge-level questions to a greater degree than teachers themselves had expected. This indicates that the tests were not aligned with the curriculum, which required higher-cognitive processes.	Broekkamp, Van Hout-Wolters, Van den Bergh, & Rijlaarsdam, 2004
♦ A study examined the variance in student achievement when taking into account the content contained in the curriculum and the cognitive levels contained in the curriculum, and then considered both content and cognitive level. When both content and cognitive level were considered, more of the class achievement gains could be explained than when the researchers considered only content or only cognitive level.	Gamoran, Poerter, Smithson, & White, 1997
♦ A study that examined the science achievement of eighth grade students found that when students were exposed to the content that students were expected to learn, they performed significantly better than did students who were not exposed to the content they were expected to learn, as measured by an end-of-unit test.	Wang, 1998

How Does a Teacher Ensure That Assessments Are Aligned with Learning Objectives?

When creating a unit of study and a summative assessment of student learning, two key factors must be considered: the (1) subject matter and (2) the thinking level required. Many times when creating an assessment a teacher might attend to the subject matter but not attend as closely to how the student will engage with the subject matter. For example, a student studying the states of matter in physical science can examine this subject matter from many different thinking levels. For example, the student might describe the physical phase changes of the states of matter, such as water, on a lower level and then distinguish between the physical properties water and water's chemical properties. One requires a basic understanding of solids, liquids, and gases, whereas the other requires a higher thinking level as the student differentiates between physical and chemical properties. It is important for teacher-made tests to reflect both the content and thinking level demanded in the curriculum and in classroom instruction. This is essentially content validity.

One way to address content validity is to develop a test blueprint or a table of specifications when creating a test. The purpose of the test blueprint is to describe the content covered on the test and to ensure that the content is adequately sampled on the test.[6] The steps[7] involved in creating a sample test blueprint include:

- *Step 1*—Deciding which instructional objectives will be tested in a paper/pencil format.

  This step links the test with curriculum and instruction. A teacher can examine lesson plans and ensure that the test content matches the instructional content. The teacher must also make decisions concerning which instructional objectives can be tested using a paper/pencil format. Some instructional objectives cannot be tested using all item formats. For example, it would be nearly impossible to test whether a student could "demonstrate appropriate performance behavior"[8] when attending a musical concert using a paper/pencil format. The best way to assess this instructional objective would be through an observation of the student at a musical concert. However, knowledge of appropriate performance behavior could be measured through a multiple choice question.

- *Step 2*—Making a table of specifications.

  A table of specifications consists of mapping the content, the thinking level required, and the number of items within each cell. The content and thinking level required are gleaned from the instructional objectives. The *Table of Specifications* template in Figure 4.2 provides an example of how a teacher might plan for an assessment that matches both the content and the thinking level (a reproducible blank copy of the *Table of Specifications* template can be found in Part II). The left hand column details the content to be assessed. The row across the top details the thinking level required. The numbers in the boxes indicate the number of items that assess the content and the thinking level required.

Figure 4.2 connects the items on the test with the content and thinking level for a fourth grade test on Ancient Greece. The content and thinking levels were gleaned from the instructional objectives. The test is based on a one-week unit on Ancient Greece that is aligned to established standards, such as state or school curriculum. In examining the sample test blueprint, note the emphasis placed on the contributions of the Ancient Greeks to modern-day society and on the similarities and differences between Ancient Greece and the United States. Eight of the twenty items on the test address this particular content. To examine the true validity (appropriateness) of this test, we would need to examine the relative emphasis the instructional objective received in instruction. The *Table of Specifications* provides a simple, quick way to ensure that the content of the unit studied is matched with the content on the test in both subject matter and thinking level required.

Figure 4.2. Sample Completed Table of Specifications

4th Grade Level Unit on Ancient Greece

Content/Subject Matter	Number of Items Within Thinking Level Required			
	Knows	Understands	Applies	Total
Physical characteristics of Greece	2	1	1	4
Interpreting a map	0	1	2	3
Human characteristics of Greece	1	1	0	2
Human–environment interaction in Ancient Greece	1	1	1	3
Contributions of Ancient Greece to modern-day society (i.e., government, art, architecture, and sports)	2	2	0	4
Similarities and differences between Ancient Greece and the United States	1	1	2	4
Total Questions	7	7	6	20

By Creating Rubrics That Communicate Expectations to Students

Why Should Teachers Create Rubrics When Assessing Students?

Assessment is for everyone. Teachers are not the sole dispensers of feedback in classrooms. Increasingly student ownership of their learning and work products is being recognized as a vital component for success. Yet, ownership does not necessarily mean that students inherently know effective ways to evaluate their projects. Rubrics are a means to encourage both student ownership as well as grounding student evaluation of the work. Developing and using rubrics can have many positive effects in the classroom. These include:

♦ Increased student involvement in the assessment process, which makes assessment part of learning rather than a measure of the end result.[9]

♦ More reliable scoring of tasks as the teacher uses a rubric with specified criteria rather than scoring tasks without any specified criteria.[10]

♦ Decreased time spent grading by the teacher as the rubric focuses the grading.

What Does Research Say About the Connection Between Using Rubrics in the Classroom and Student Learning?

The use of rubrics has many positive effects, which, in turn, positively affect student learning. So, although the research here does not directly link the use of rubrics to student achievement, it does provide some indication that the use of rubrics positively impacts student learning. For example, consider the research studies in Figure 4.3.

Figure 4.3. Use of Rubrics and Student Learning

Related Findings	Citation
♦ A study examined the effects of peer-evaluation and self-evaluation on student learning. The researchers found that students who self-evaluated their work using a rubric improved dramatically. Researchers also found high correlations between student self-ratings and teacher ratings of student performance.	Sadler & Good, 2006
♦ Teacher training in use of rubrics can impact accuracy in accurately scoring student work, which leads to a more valid interpretation of student learning.	Schafer, Swanson, Bene, & Newberry, 2001

How Does a Teacher Develop Rubrics That Clearly Communicate Expectations to Students?

Depending on the author, rubrics have different names from "descriptive summarization" to "behaviorally-anchored rubric." Some authors object to rubrics having grades attached to them,[11] while others view the practice of numerical summarization as a "straightforward and commonly used approach to summarizing performance."[12] Essentially, rubrics are a means of communicating expectations associated with a range of performance levels of students and then using those expectations to assess student's work. The decision as to which work products should receive grades as part of the assessment belongs to the teacher.

Bare Bones Basic Rubric

A rubric goes beyond a 1 to 4 rating or labels (e.g., exemplary, satisfactory, needs improvement, and unsatisfactory). It provides a description for what each item means. Figure 4.4 is an example of a very general rubric. The rubric could be applied to virtually any assignment in any content area. In essence, it serves as a substitute for a numerical or letter grade by providing a description of each level.

Figure 4.4. Sample Generic Rubric

Best Work	Better Work	Good Work	Poor Work
All parts of the assignment are complete with accurate and exceptionally well-constructed responses.	All aspects of the assignment are complete with consistently solid responses.	Most of the assignment is complete demonstrating an understanding of most of the material.	The assignment is incomplete or demonstrates a lack of understanding of the material.

Tailored to the Assignment Objectives Rubric

A more informative approach is to identify the various attributes of an assignment and develop a rubric for each attribute. For example, consider household chores in Figure 4.5 (page 72). By providing feedback on discrete items, students have a better idea of areas in which they can improve as well as what the "next step" up of performance resembles.

Rubric Construction 101

The *Rubric Development Template* available in Part II of this book provides a guide that you can use to create your own rubrics or involve your students in creating a rubric for an assignment. To construct a rubric:

1. *Determine the level of specificity desired.* If it is a general one-size-fits-most-assignments rubric the first step is done. If it is a more tailored rubric, identify the key components of the assignment that will be rated. Each component should be distinct.

2. *Determine how many levels are desired in the rubric.* Usually the number is three to five. In the chores rubric example (Figure 4.5), there were two levels of acceptable performance (i.e., well done and good) and two levels of unacceptable performance (i.e., needs improvement and unsatisfactory).

3. *Write a description for each level.* It is often easiest to start with the expected level of successful performance (e.g., good) and then focus on the lowest level of performance (e.g., unsatisfactory). Finally consider what would define exceptional performance as well was needs improvement.

Figure 4.5. Sample Completed Rubric

Chore	Well Done *In addition to meeting the "Good" standard...*	Good	Needs Improvement	Unsatisfactory
Taking care of the dog	Extra time was spent brushing the dog's coat and/or walking the dog.	The dog was fed in the morning and the water bowl was refilled during the day as needed.	The dog was fed and watered in the morning.	The dog was not fed and/or watered until a reminder was given.
Cleaning the bathroom	Hard to reach surfaces were dusted (e.g., s-curves on the toilet base, top of doors, and top of the shower).	The tub, toilet, mirror, and sink with vanity were cleaned appropriately, including the mopping of the floor.	The tub, toilet, mirror, and sink with vanity were cleaned.	The bathroom was spot cleaned.
Vacuuming	The crevice between the floorboard and the carpet was vacuumed.	All carpets were vacuumed, including under tables and movable chairs.	Most of the carpets were vacuumed, although it appears some spots were missed.	Not all the carpets were vacuumed and/or streaks were left on the carpet because the bag was not changed.

By Providing Feedback to Students That Moves Their Learning Forward

Why Should Teachers Focus on Providing Feedback?

The focus on formative assessment in recent years has changed how we view the purposes and uses of assessment in the classroom.[13] Instead of assessment serving merely to provide a summary judgment of student performance, assessment is now being seen as a vehicle *for* learning. Instruction and assessment are viewed as integral to each other *rather than* separate activities that occur at separate points in the classroom.[14] Within this context, the effective teacher:

♦ Recognizes the connection between instruction and assessment and uses daily classroom activities to assess and monitor student learning;

♦ Identifies student strengths and weaknesses and pinpoints where students are now and where they need to be;

♦ Focuses on strategies to close the gap between where the students are now and where they need to be;

♦ Provides feedback to students on their progress, both in terms of daily activities and overall progress; and,

♦ Helps students learn how to assess themselves and provide constructive feedback to peers using established criteria for the task.[15]

Consider the conceptual model of feedback offered in Figure 4.6 and the example in the sidebar. In the model, a teacher plans a learning experience that is aligned to classroom instructional objectives, local school district curriculum, as well as state standards. Feedback is provided by teachers and by the students themselves through self-assessment or peer assessment. The arrows that flow from the feedback to the student response and learning experiences are probably the most important aspect of this model. Students use feedback to modify their responses to the learning experiences and teachers use feedback to modify the learning experiences based on students' responses.

A teacher may engage students in a mini-lesson on presenting an argument in a persuasive essay. The teacher has students use what they have learned to outline an argument to present. The student then responds to the learning experiences. Sometimes this response is oral, such as answering a question posed by a teacher; at other times, the response is written, such as the example of students outlining an argument to use in writing a persuasive essay. Finally, the student receives feedback based on some type of criteria.

Figure 4.6. Relationship of Feedback to the Learning Process

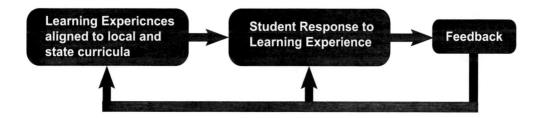

What Does Research Say About the Connection Between Feedback and Student Learning?

Feedback has come to be viewed as an instructional technique that can have tremendous impact on student achievement.[16] In fact, in a review of research studies related to factors that impact student achievement, feedback surpassed socioeconomic status in the effects on student learning.[17] One study found a significant, positive relationship between the feedback provided to students and the quality of student writing.[18] Reviews of research related to effective feedback practices focus on three key aspects, which are shown in Figure 4.7.

Figure 4.7. Elements Related to Effective Feedback and Student Learning

Element	Description
Timely	Students who receive feedback close to the assessment activity perform better than students who receive feedback at a later time. However, some feedback may be more appropriately given at a later time, such as when students are learning new concepts and need to grapple with the information before receiving feedback—timing is the key.[19]
Specific	Effective teachers provide feedback that is specific enough so that students understand how to improve.[20]
Constructive	Feedback that focuses on improvement, is correct and neutral in nature, and is based on specified criteria is indicative of practices of effective teachers.[21]

Providing feedback to students in the classroom is similar to a swim coach providing feedback to swimmers. The coach has experiences with swimming, knows the rules related to various strokes involved in swimming, and understands the art of swimming. Likewise, a teacher has experiences with the skills and knowledge of a particular content area, has an understanding of the criteria used to determine whether students have demonstrated achievement of the necessary skills and knowledge, and her expertise allows her to share the art of the content, not just the science. Figure 4.8 looks at the analogy of the swim coach and the teacher in relation to the three key aspects of feedback.

Teachers provide feedback on a minute-by-minute, day-by-day, week-by-week basis. The quality of that feedback is what makes the difference between feedback that improves student learning and feedback that negatively impacts a student's motivation and, thus, academic progress.[22]

How Can a Teacher Analyze Feedback Provided to Determine Whether Effective Feedback Is Being Given?

This section offers a way to examine your own assessment practices in light of recommendations from the research related to elements and key aspects of effective feedback. The *Feedback Analysis Template* offers a way to critically analyze your own feedback (a blank, reproducible of the *Feedback Analysis Template* can be found in Part II).

How to Use the Feedback Analysis Template

Collect at least ten student papers from at least five separate assignments that have been already been assessed and are ready to hand back to students. This collection method works well primarily for teachers who send home weekly folders or require students to keep assignments in a notebook. Other teachers may find it useful to copy

Figure 4.8. Key Aspects of Feedback

Feedback Aspect	Swim Coach	Classroom Teacher
Timely	The coach stops the swimmer and provides feedback on how to move the legs during the butterfly. The student subsequently incorporates the feedback as he continues the lap. However, if the feedback is provided the following week without an opportunity to incorporate the feedback, the swimmer will most likely forget and will continue to swim the butterfly incorrectly.	A student who receives feedback on an argument outlined for a persuasive essay as she is working on the outline or the next day will be able to use the feedback to change the outline prior to writing the essay.
Specific	A swimmer who is told that his breast stroke needs some improvement lacks specific information on what to improve. By contrast, a swimmer who is told that this legs need to snap together at a faster and stronger pace has more specific information about how and what to improve.	A student who receives the comment "redo" on the outline for a persuasive essay with no other information is at a loss—What is it that needs to be redone? By contrast, a student who receives feedback that the argument points need supporting details has more specific information.
Constructive	A swim coach tells a swimmer that he was disqualified in the breast stroke event. A better response to improve the swimmer's performance would have been to remind him that he must touch two hands at the turns and the finish rather than the finish only.	A teacher who writes the letter grade "C−" on the essay outline has given feedback, but the feedback lacks specificity and does not point the student in the right direction. However, if the teacher provides feedback that states "remember to provide supporting details to support each argument point," she gives the student constructive ways to improve and that are related to the criteria on writing a good persuasive essay.

ten student papers from each of the next five assignments that are made (but not make changes in the assessment practices).

For each assignment, in the first column on the blackline master, write down what the assignment was. In the second and third columns, indicate with a simple "yes" or "no" whether criteria had been developed for assessing the work and whether the criteria had been shared with students. In the next column, indicate whether any written feedback was provided to students.

The next series of columns relate to the nature of any feedback provided. First, review the feedback and indicate whether it was positive, negative, or neutral. Then, think about whether the feedback was specific to the criteria and pointed the students in the right direction, in other words, whether the feedback was constructive. After collecting at least ten assignments and analyzing the feedback, total the columns to reveal your own assessment practices.

Discussion of Sample Completed Feedback Analysis

Take a look at the sample provided in Figure 4.9. Perry Odical is a high school science teacher. He decides to analyze assignments he has given his students to develop and carry out a science project. Perry collects six assignments, which are listed on the chart. The assignments show that Perry is using modeling to help students carry out their own projects. Students analyze a fictional science experiment and then begin to create their own.

From the chart Perry completed, a few "ahas" emerge. Perry provided students with the criteria for the overall assignment as they were working on the final report rather than incrementally. Thus, they knew the big assessment picture but not the criteria for each individual component. Perry provides feedback to his students, but it is all positive. You may ask, what's wrong with all positive feedback? The last two columns give us the answer. Perry's comments are specific, but not constructive. For example, he may note, "I really like how you depicted your information." All his comments praise student efforts; none of them challenge students to extend their thinking or to think about data in different ways. Finally, because Perry did not develop criteria for the first four assignments, he cannot provide focused feedback.

By Using Assessment Data to Set Student Achievement Goals[23]

Why Should Teachers Use Assessment Data to Set Student Achievement Goals?

In essence, if we do not use data to set student achievement goals than we are like an athlete preparing for a race without knowing how much we need to prepare and even what we are preparing for in the first place. Every four years, the Winter Olympics keep spectators around the world on the edge of their seats as they watch athletes from around the globe compete for the ultimate prize in sports—the Olympic Gold Medal. Although not all athletes achieve the Gold, some win a Silver or Bronze medal, and others are pleased to just be among those participating. All accomplishments are recognized.

As spectators we witness the culmination of years of hard work and perseverance. What we do not see at the Olympics are the hours of practice, the sacrifice of time with family, and the daily, weekly, monthly, and yearly regimen required to reach this pinnacle within the world of sports.

Figure 4.9. Sample Completed Feedback Analysis Template

Assignment	Feedback Provided Y/N	Criteria Developed for Assignment Y/N	Criteria for Assignment Shared with Students Y/N	Nature of Feedback +	Nature of Feedback –	Nature of Feedback N	Specific Feedback Provided Y/N	Constructive Feedback Provided Y/N
Analysis of a fictional science project idea and description	Y	N	N	✓			N	N
Individual student science project idea and description	Y	N	N	✓			N	N
Analysis of fictional science experiment data	Y	N	N	✓			N	N
Individual student analysis of experiment data	Y	N	N	✓			N	N
Analysis of fictional science project report	Y	Y	Y	✓			Y	N
Individual student science project report	Y	Y	Y	✓			Y	N
Totals	Y=6 N=0	Y=2 N=4	Y=2 N=4	6	0	0	Y=2 N=4	Y=0 N=6

As educators we, too, strive for the ultimate goal—for all students to achieve. We begin with the end in mind. To understand what it will take to reach the goal, teachers must examine where students begin—much like athletes record how fast they can ski in the downhill or how well they can maneuver the snowboard as a baseline for what they must do to improve.

Once we have established a goal that is based on how students perform in the beginning and where they must end up, we strategize how to help students to get there based on what we know works. Again, Olympic athletes do much the same. The downhill skier does not only ski downhill continuously to practice. He or she may also run, lift weights, and perform myriad other activities in order to reach the ultimate goal. Teachers go through the same process in planning instructional activities that help their students achieve.

What Does Research Say About the Connection Between Setting Student Achievement Goals and Student Learning?

Research shows that practices associated academic goal setting can have a positive impact on student achievement.[24] The research studies summarized in Figure 4.10 support elements related to student achievement goal setting.

Figure 4.10. Relationship Between Learning and Goal Setting

Element	Description
Mastery learning	The idea of mastery learning is closely associated with academic goal setting. In mastery learning, students are constantly assessed to determine their progress toward a goal—mastery of certain content or skills. Teachers set goals based on students' current needs and assess progress along the way, making adjustments as needed. Students who are taught using mastery learning strategies achieve one standard deviation above students taught using conventional methods. Thus, students who were taught using mastery learning achieved at the 84th percentile, whereas students taught using conventional methods were at the 50th percentile.[25]
School improvement	Research also supports school districts' use of data to make decisions and set goals for school improvement as leading to better student outcomes.[26] Studies of high-performing school districts have found that these districts encourage teachers, schools, and the district as a whole to make decisions based on student achievement or progress data. They also train teachers on how to use assessments to guide instruction.[27]
Feedback	The foundation for goal setting is assessment, with feedback both for the students and the teacher playing a critical role.[28] In particular, feedback is used to correct errors in logic. Teachers engage in assessing, providing corrective feedback, and adjusting instruction. Feedback that focuses on improvement, is correct and neutral in nature, and is based on specified criteria is indicative of practices of effective teachers.[29]

Although Olympic athletes have only one chance at winning in a particular year, they have other chances to demonstrate their abilities in many other venues. Students, too, deserve that second chance to demonstrate what they know and are capable of. When teachers focus on instruction with the beginning and the end in mind, then students, schools, and districts improve.

How Does a Teacher Develop Goals That Improve Student Learning?

Student achievement goal setting involves a multistep process in which teachers examine where their students are now and where they should be at the end of the year. Based on the gap that may exist, teachers set goals for improved student achievement. A goal cannot be attained without the development of strategies; therefore, once the goal is set, teachers develop strategies for reaching it. The goal may be used as a professional development tool whereby teachers seek not only to improve the academic achievement of their students, but their own practice as well. For example, a teacher may choose to focus the goal on improving reading instruction and to do so may take a graduate-level course on reading across the content areas so that she can infuse reading instruction in social studies, science, and mathematics. Figure 4.11 (page 80) provides a model for how the student-achievement goal-setting process works.

Developing the Student Achievement Goal

Developing the goal involves first examining the context in which the teacher works. For example, a goal for teachers who work with students with multiple physical challenges will look different from that of teachers who work with students in the general school population.

- ◆ *Setting*—The setting should include the number of students and any other pertinent information such as the number of students on free and reduced-price lunch or the number of students who have individualized education plans (IEPs). A description of the context in which the teacher works informs the person reading the goal of whether the goal is appropriate.

- ◆ *Focus area*—The focus area refers to the content or subject area on which the goal will be based. This decision is informed by overall strengths and weaknesses of the students. For example, a social studies teacher may decide to focus on historical analysis as students may have a weakness in this area. The focus is based on both the content and the students' needs.

- ◆ *Baseline data*—Baseline data are important as they provide the basis for the goal. Baseline data can include, for example, student performance on the Dynamic Indicator of Basic Early Literacy Skills (DIBELS) assessment in September. These baseline data provide an elementary teacher with information regarding students' prereading skills. The DIBELS assessment administered in September serves as a preassessment.

Figure 4.11. Student-Achievement Goal-Setting Process[30]

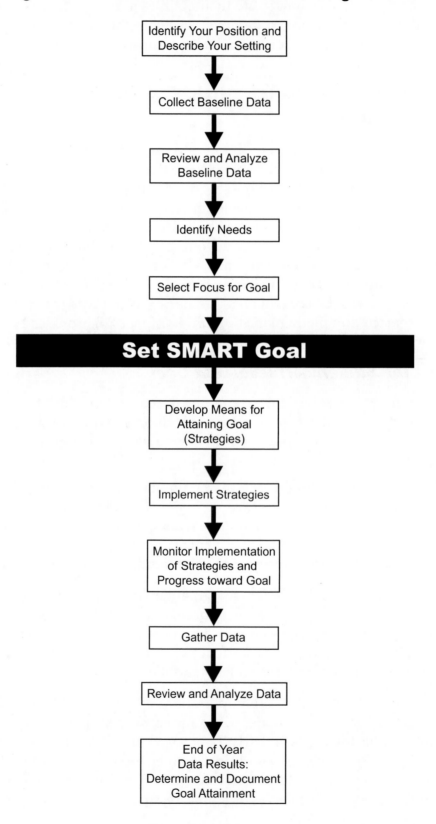

Identify Your Position and
Describe Your Setting

↓

Collect Baseline Data

↓

Review and Analyze
Baseline Data

↓

Identify Needs

↓

Select Focus for Goal

↓

Set SMART Goal

↓

Develop Means for
Attaining Goal
(Strategies)

↓

Implement Strategies

↓

Monitor Implementation
of Strategies and
Progress toward Goal

↓

Gather Data

↓

Review and Analyze Data

↓

End of Year
Data Results:
Determine and Document
Goal Attainment

♦ *Goal statement*—Once the teacher knows where the students are, he can set the goal for where students should be at the end of the year. Goals should be SMART. Figure 4.12 defines the SMART criteria. That is, *S*pecific, *M*easurable, *A*ppropriate, *A*ttainable, and *T*ime-bound. See sidebar for an example of a SMART goal.

Figure 4.12. SMART Criteria Used for Goal Setting[31]

Specific
The goal is focused such as by content area and by learners' needs.

Measurable
An appropriate instrument/ measure is selected to assess the goal.

Appropriate
The goal is clearly related to the role and responsibilities of the instructional professional.

Realistic
The goal is attainable by the instructional professional.

Time-bound
The goal is contained to a single school year.

During the current school year, my sixth-grade physical education students will increase performance by an average of 20% on each of the Presidential Fitness Test subareas.

Specific: The goal is focused on physical education, specifically the Presidential Fitness sub areas and a 20% average gain.

Measurable: The teacher identified Presidential Fitness Test to be used to assess goal.

Appropriate: The teacher teaches the content and skills contained in the Presidential Fitness Tests.

Realistic: The goal of increasing student performance by 20% is realistic. It is not out of reach and yet not too easy.

Time-bound: Goal attainment can be addressed by the end of the year with the final Presidential Fitness Test.

♦ *Means for attaining the goal*—Strategy development is the next step in the process. Strategies should be specific; that is, detailing how the goal is to be accomplished. Let's take the physical education teacher's goal as an example. Consider the strategies below:

• Have students set daily activity goals for an 8-week period.

• Once a month test on the Presidential Fitness subtests.

• Incorporate student goal setting based on Presidential Fitness goals.

The goal of this teacher is not to have every student achieve the Presidential Fitness Award—that would not be attainable as students who reach this achievement are in the 85th percentile. However, the teacher does want students to increase physical activity and in doing so increase their performance on the Presidential Fitness Test. The strategies help students reach the goal of increasing their performance on the subtests.

♦ *Mid-year review*—Throughout the year, the strategies and student progress toward the goal should be monitored. For example, the physical education teacher is testing the students once a month on the Presidential Fitness subtests. Therefore, the students and the teacher can monitor progress toward the goal.

♦ *End-of-year review*—At the end of the year, the teacher administers the post-assessment. The information gained here provides the basis for evaluating whether the goal was attained. Figure 4.13 shows a completed *Student Achievement Goal Setting Form* (a blank reproducible of the *Student Achievement Goal Setting Form* is available in Part II).

Summary

In this chapter, we provide four ways to enhance the assessment process in order to make assessment part of teaching and learning rather than a linear process in which we teach–assess–teach–assess. These four ways do not encompass the *most* effective ways of assessing nor do they take into account the myriad factors in assessing student achievement, but they are, indeed, supported by research as having a positive impact on student achievement. The key is to focus on both assessment *of* learning and assessment *for* learning so that we use best practice in determining whether students have achieved learning goals and in determining how to use student achievement data to adjust instruction and meet student needs. Some of these strategies to address both the *of* and *for* includes strategies that:

♦ Align curriculum and instruction with assessment so that assessments provide teachers with information they need;

♦ Use rubrics to define criteria for success and involve students in the assessment process;

♦ Provide feedback to students so that they know how they are doing and what they need to do to improve; and

♦ Set goals for student achievement that meet both the needs of the curriculum and the needs of the students.

Figure 4.13. Sample Completed Student-Achievement Goal-Setting Form[32]

Teacher's Name: <u>Marcus Rios</u>

School: <u>Sunnyvale Middle School</u>   Job Title: <u>P.E. Teacher</u>   School Year: <u>Current</u>

I. Setting (Describe the population and special learning circumstances)	I teach in an urban elementary school of 824 students. 45% of the students are on free and reduced-price lunch. I teach 6th, 7th, and 8th grade students.
II. Content/Subject/Field Area (The area/topic addressed based on learner achievement, data analysis, or observational data)	The area I will address is student progress on the Presidential Fitness Test. Presidential Fitness Test goals are based on students who score at the 85th percentile or better on each subarea.
III. Baseline Data (What the current data show)	A pretest of each subarea shows that a majority of my 6th-grade students failed to reach the benchmarks in the Presidential Fitness Test. ☒ Data attached (Preassessment of Presidential Fitness subtests)
IV. Goal Statement (Describe what you want learners/program to accomplish)	In the 2009-10 school year, my 6th-grade students will improve on each of the Presidential Fitness subtests by an average of 20%.

V. Means for Attaining Goal (Activities used to accomplish the goal)

Strategy	Measurable By	Target Date
Have students set daily activity goals for an 8-week period	Student completion of daily activity logs	December
Once a month test on the Presidential Fitness Test subtests	Planning documents and student score records	Ongoing (October–April)
Incorporate student goal setting	Students setting goals in each sub-area and tracking progress Student completion of graphs after each subtesting	Ongoing (October–April)

VI. Mid-Year Review (Describe goal progress and other relevant data)	
VII. End-of-Year Data Results (Accomplishments at the end of year)	☐ Data attached

Notes

1   Stiggins, 2002.

2   Black, Harrison, Lee, Marshall, & Wiliam, 2003.

3   Brown, 2002, p. 185.

4   Airasian & Miranda, 2002, p. 253.

5   Rowan, Harrison, & Hayes, 2005.

6   Gronlund, 2006; Hogan, 2007; Stiggins, 1997; Notar, Zuelke, Wilson, & Yunker, 2004.

7   Steps adapted from Gareis & Grant, 2008; Gronlund, 2006.

8   Virginia Department of Education, 2006.

9   Sadler & Good, 2006.

10 Gareis & Grant, 2008.

11 Brown, 2002.

12 Airasian, 1994.

13 Hargreaves, 2005.

14 Gareis & Grant, 2008.

15 Covino & Iwanicki, 1996; Noonan & Duncan, 2005; Wharton-McDonald, Pressley, & Hampston, 1998.

16 Black et al., 2003.

17 Hattie & Timperley, 2007.

18 Matsumura, Patthey-Chavez, Valdes, & Garnier, 2002.

19 Bangert-Downs, Kulik, Kulick, & Morgan, 1991.

20 Walberg, 1984.

21 Covino & Iwanicki, 1996; Marzano, 2006; Singham, 2001.

22 Marzano, 2006.

23 For a more in-depth study of student achievement goal setting see Stronge, J.H., & Grant, L.W. (2009). *Student achievement goal setting: Using assessment data to improve teaching and learning.* Larchmont, NY: Eye On Education.

24 Fuchs, Deno, & Mirkin, 1984.

25 Bloom, 1984.

26 Cawelti, 2004.

27 Snipes, Doolittle, & Herlihy, 2002.

28 Guskey, 2003.

29 Covino & Iwanicki, 1996; Marzano, 2006; Singham, 2001.

30 Adapted from Stronge, J.H., & Grant, L.W. (2009). *Student achievement goal setting: Using assessment data to improve teaching and learning.* Larchmont, NY: Eye On Education.

31   Reprinted from Stronge, J.H., & Grant, L.W. (2009). *Student achievement goal setting: Using assessment data to improve teaching and learning.* Larchmont, NY: Eye On Education.

32   Form printed in Stronge, J.H., & Grant, L.W. (2009). Stronge, J.H., & Grant, L.W. (2009). *Student achievement goal setting: Using assessment data to improve teaching and learning.* Larchmont, NY: Eye On Education.

5

Conclusion

> **teach** (tech) **taught, teaching 1.** to show or help to learn how to do something; **4.** to provide with knowledge, insight, etc.; cause to know, understand
>
> **learn** (lurn) **learned learning 1.** to get knowledge or (a subject) or skill by study, experience, instruction, etc. **2.** to come to know
>
> *Webster's New World Dictionary of the American Language*

Teaching and *learning*—these two terms are inextricably linked. If teaching doesn't result in learning, then what is the point of a child spending 180 or more days per academic year in the classroom?[1] The imparting of knowledge supposes a two-way communication. A teacher's success in imparting knowledge and skills is only as great as the degree to which the student gained the knowledge and skills. Indeed, the teacher creates the "experience" and the "study" by which students learn but, ultimately, if students don't learn then has the teacher really taught?[2]

It is precisely this connection between teaching and learning to which this book is devoted. In this concluding chapter for Part I of *Planning, Instruction, and Assessment: Effective Teaching Practices*, we address the following key questions regarding teaching and learning in terms of teacher quality:

♦ How is instructional planning an important component of teacher quality?

♦ How is instructional delivery an important component of teacher quality?

♦ How is student assessment an important component of teacher quality?

♦ What is the connection among planning, instruction, and assessment?

♦ What is the heart of learning?

In an effort to analyze and explore the teacher's instructional practices, we devoted the bulk (Chapters 2 to 4) of *Planning, Instruction, and Assessment: Effective Teaching Practices* to address each of three critical attributes: (1) instructional planning, (2) instructional delivery, and (3) student assessment. As evidence behind the salience of these three teacher quality attributes, we offer a summary here.

How Is Instructional Planning an Important Component of Teacher Quality?

Before an action takes place, a solid plan of action is essential. Thus, instructional planning is an integral part—and precursor—of teaching. Thorough planning should:

♦ Show professionalism;[3]

♦ Demonstrate a consideration of the teaching context and the students;

♦ Allow a teacher to predict possible problems and think about how to address them; and, ultimately,

♦ Enhance student achievement.[4]

When teachers don't plan—or don't plan well—even their students become aware of this failing: "Pupils do notice if a teacher is ill prepared for teaching…pupils may feel if the teacher is not prepared for teaching, why should they study hard and be accountable for doing well in school."[5]

Planning is influenced by myriad factors, including a teacher's understanding of the content and the students' needs. But, planning also is impacted by a teachers' expertise, which may or may not correlate with experience. Applying the idea of a continuum to teacher quality, teachers may fall along the continuum from *novice* to *master* as demonstrated in Figure 5.1.

Figure 5.1. Continuum of Teacher Quality

Planning for instruction is influenced by this continuum of teachers' expertise. Novice teachers often are described as inefficient, time consuming, rigid, linear, and ignoring the individual needs of students. Additionally, novice teachers spend more time learning subject matter and selecting appropriate activities than master teachers.[6] By comparison, master teacher planning is described as fluid and complex, with multiple ideas for lessons. Expert teacher planners build multiple contingencies based on student performance. Moreover, the experienced teacher has a repertoire of strategies to use with different content.[7] Given this type of continuum, expertise in planning requires time, practice, experience, and growth.[8]

How Is Instructional Delivery an Important Component of Teacher Effectiveness?

Frameworks for Instructional Delivery

Instructional delivery is such a broad and deep subject to attempt to summarize, perhaps a useful beginning would be to consider appropriate frameworks for instructional effectiveness. As one such framework for what good teachers should know and be able to do in terms of instructional delivery, consider the National Board for Professional Teaching Standards' (NBPTS) *Proposition 2: Teachers Know the Subjects They Teach and How to Teach Those Subjects to Students.*[9]

1. National Board Certified Teachers (NBCTs) have mastery over the subject(s) they teach. They have a deep understanding of the history, structure, and real-world applications of the subject.

2. They have skill and experience in teaching it, and they are very familiar with the skills gaps and preconceptions students may bring to the subject.

3. They are able to use diverse instructional strategies to teach for understanding.

Another useful framework for instructional delivery is provided by Interstate New Teacher Assessment and Support Consortium (INTASC). INTASC is a consortium of state departments of education and national organizations whose purpose is to reform the preparation and licensing of teachers. This consortium recognizes the critical focus on the act of teaching. For example, consider Standard 4 which focuses on a teacher's knowledge of the appropriate use of a variety of instructional strategies.

Standard 4: Multiple Instructional Strategies

The teacher understands and uses a variety of instructional strategies to encourage student development of critical thinking, problem solving, and performance skills.[10]

Indeed, educational organizations that certify master teachers and organizations committed to the improvement of teacher preparation programs underscore the critical need for quality instruction.

The Practice of Instructing

Within the various frameworks of effective teachers' instructional delivery, the real proof of effectiveness is impact on students' learning. We do know from a clear line of research that quality instructional delivery leads to increases in students' understanding and retention of material when the lessons actively involve them.[11] Also, hands-on and inquiry-learning approaches offer teachers ways to deliver instruction that are tailored to student learning needs and, thus, enables them to interact with the curriculum.[12] Additionally, research shows that quality teachers ask questions designed to support student learning, assess student understanding, and enhance the overall instructional process. These teachers not only plan key questions to pose, but also thoughtfully wait and consider student responses and questions.[13]

Another key attribute of quality instructional delivery—teaching for meaning—requires classroom teachers to have a sense of the "big picture" in order to organize the content within the larger conceptual framework. Teaching for meaning supports students understanding a concept as opposed to fragmented inputs.[14]

These key attributes, among others, impact quality instruction in the classroom. The treatment of instructional delivery in this book in no way encompasses the complexity of instructional delivery and the myriad strategies that have been shown to be effective in increasing student achievement. It does, however, offer ways to think about how to make instruction challenging, engaging, and meaningful—that's quality teaching!

How Is Student Assessment an Important Component of Teacher Quality?

Policy Frameworks for Assessment

Another essential teacher quality is the ability to use assessment information to make appropriate judgments about student learning and to make appropriate instructional decisions to move student learning forward. Both the INTASC[15] and the National Council for Accreditation of Teacher Education (NCATE) recognize the importance of teacher-preparation programs equipping new teachers with skills in developing and using assessments and interpreting assessment data.[16] Additionally, the Partnership for 21st Century Skills views assessment as necessary to ensure that students develop the knowledge and skills to be successful in the future.[17] As suggested by these influential policy groups, effective assessment is critical to teaching and learning.

The Practice of Assessment

In teaching and learning, assessment has been viewed as an integral part of this equation. But, what has been less clear is *how* assessment fits into the teaching and learning process. Is it something done at the end of instruction? Is it something done during instruction? Is it something done prior to instruction? Oftentimes, the view of assessment reflects the first question, placing assessment at the end of a linear progression of planning, teaching, and assessing. However, we now know that assessment is so much more and indeed improved assessment practices leads to improved student learning.[18] As discussed in Chapter 4, assessment involves focusing on all three questions: assessing before the instructional process, during the instructional process, and after the instructional process. Each point of assessment serves its own important purpose in providing teachers with information they need to make appropriate judgments and providing students with information they need to improve.

Possessing some or all of the "right qualities" described above does not necessarily make a great teacher. While we can quite adeptly describe the key qualities of outstanding teachers, there is a more personal side to knowing teacher quality. Thus, we must consider not only the defining qualities of outstanding teachers, but also how we interact with and view quality on a more personal level. The companion book, *The Supportive Learning Environment: Effective Teacher Practices*, focuses on those aspects of the teacher's work that supports the teaching and learning process, including the importance of developing and maintaining caring relationships with students.

What Is the Connection Among Planning, Instruction, and Assessment?

When we consider what virtually all quality teachers do that most directly impacts students' learning and lives, we note three classroom variables:

♦ Instructional planning;

♦ Instructional delivery; and

♦ Student assessment.

These three factors are highly intertwined and, in reality, virtually impossible to unravel. Consider Figure 5.2 in which the relationships among the three are depicted as distinctive, yet highly interrelated pieces.

Figure 5.2. The Interrelationship Among Planning, Instruction, and Assessment

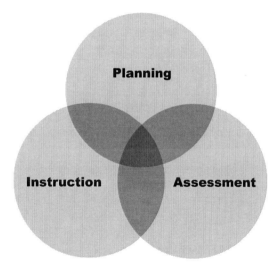

Although planning, instruction, and assessment include distinct skills and processes, an effective teacher knows how these critical aspects of teaching and learning work together to improve student learning. The effective teacher does not view each element separately but rather as a composite picture of what students should know and be able to do, the activities that students will engage in to get there, and how the teacher and the students will know how they are doing along the way and when they meet the mark set. It is this interrelationship among these three teacher practices that help define teacher quality—especially in terms of classroom practices and direct impact on student learning.

What Is the Heart of Learning?

Interacting with a Quality Teacher

Hopefully, all of us have had one or more outstanding teachers who made a significant, positive impact in our lives. Such an educator represents the sum total of a quality teacher for each of us in a highly personalized manner. Although these teachers typically do reflect the numerous positive attributes described throughout *Planning, Instruction, and Assessment: Effective Teaching Practices*, they are not wholly defined by or confined to those descriptors. Rather, we consider them to be extraordinary, quality teachers because they were extraordinary in our lives.

Considering this personal side of teacher quality, interacting with a quality teacher has been described as "…bringing distinctive life experiences and perspectives to the classroom; providing valuable role models for minority and nonminority students alike; enriching the curriculum, assessment, and school climate; and strengthening connections to parents and communities."[19] Thus, a quality teacher is one who connects with the learner and then facilitates building bridges among content, skills, and processes in a meaningful manner for the student.

Qualities in art combine to form an image just as teacher qualities come together to make up the real teacher in a given classroom. Depending on the interactions, the result may be positive, negative, or neutral. And just as artists develop over time, so do teachers. A key challenge in understanding teacher quality is that teaching revolves around a dynamic interplay of personal, pedagogical, and cultural contexts that must be combined to form a quality teacher who is a complex individual, working with equally complex and unique students.

Notes

1   Gareis & Grant, 2008.
2   Gareis & Grant, 2008.
3   Robertson & Acklam, 2000.
4   Duff, n.d.
5   Ediger, 2004, p. 197.
6   Jay, 2002; Borko & Livingston, 1989; Covino & Iwanicki, 1996.
7   Jay, 2002; Borko & Livingston, 1989; Covino & Iwanicki, 1996.
8   Covino & Iwanicki, 1996.
9   National Board for Professional Teaching Standards, 2002.
10 INTASC, 2007.
11 Committee on Increasing High School Students' Engagement and Motivation to Learn, 2004.
12 Rathunde & Csikszentmihalyi, 2005.
13 Cotton, 2001; Martin, Sexton, & Gerlovich, 2001; Stronge, Tucker & Ward, 2003.
14 Joyce & Weil, 2004.
15 INTASC, 2007.
16 National Council for Accreditation of Teacher Education, 2008.
17 Partnership for 21st Century Skills, 2007.
18 Black, Harrison, Lee, Marshall, & Wiliam, 2003.
19 USDE, 1998, p. 3.

Part II

Reproducible Resources

Reproducible Resources

Throughout the book, numerous tools have been presented relating to planning, teaching, and assessing students. Part II contains full-page blanks of the resources for purchasers of the book to copy for educational use and not-for-profit use. The resources are presented alphabetically. The matrix below provides a quick reference telling the title, the original figure number, a brief purpose, and the page number. Additionally notes relating to the use of the resource are provided as applicable.

Title	Fig. #	Purpose	Page #
Concept Attainment Lesson Plan Template	3.4	To provide teachers with a format to plan a lesson that focuses on concept development.	98
Feedback Analysis Template	4.9	To help teachers analyze the nature of feedback provided to students.	99
Inquiry-based Lesson Adaptation Template	3.13	To help teachers adapt an instructional activity for inquiry-based instruction.	100
Mining State Standards	2.2	To examine state standards to ensure that the content and thinking level required by state standards are also addressed in instruction.	101
Questioning Practices Record	3.10	To provide teachers with a way to determine questioning practices, reflect on questioning practices, and make changes in the classroom.	102
Rubric Template	4.5	To help develop a rubric to assess student progress.	103
Student Engagement Record	3.15	To provide teachers with a systematic process for collecting student engagement data and relate student engagement to instructional activities.	105
Student-Achievement Goal-Setting Form	4.13	To provide teachers with a systematic process for collecting student achievement data, setting goals, developing strategies, and monitoring goal progress and attainment.	104
Student Progress Monitoring Summary	2.10	To provide a systematic process for documenting collection of data, planned intervention, and progress monitoring.	106
Table of Specifications	4.2	To plan for assessments that align with both the content and thinking level required in standards.	107
Tiered Lesson Plan Template	2.5	To facilitate planning a lesson that is differentiated to meet the needs of learners in the classroom.	108
Technology Integration Planning	2.13	To facilitate planning for the integration of technology in the curriculum.	109

Concept Attainment Lesson Planning Template

Concepts:

Learning objectives:

Definitions, Critical Attributes, and Examples of Concepts	
Concept 1: Definition: Critical Attributes: 	Concept 1: Definition: Critical Attributes:
Examples of Concept 1: 	Examples of Concept 2:

Feedback Analysis Template

Assignment	Feedback Provided Y/N	Criteria Developed for Assignment Y/N	Criteria for Assignment Shared with Students Y/N	Nature of Feedback			Specific Feedback Provided Y/N	Constructive Feedback Provided Y/N
				+	–	N		
Totals	Y= N=	Y= N=	Y= N=				Y= N=	Y= N=

Inquiry-Based Lesson-Adaptation Template

Activity's Name:

Resources to Use:

Focus:

Justifying the Inquiry: What are learning outcomes related to the inquiry?

Building up to the Inquiry: What activities and learning experiences have students had or will have had to prepare them for the inquiry?

Thinking Through the Inquiry: What are the items and issues related to this topic?

Identifying Likely Supports Tools: What resources will I need to support the inquiry? What resources will likely be needed by students?

Identifying Potential Barriers: What barriers may exist in completing the inquiry lesson?

Completing the Inquiry: How will students know that they've arrived at a stopping point? How will I provide feedback on the students' inquiry process?

Considering the Potential Investment: How long will the inquiry take? Is it worth it?

Reflecting on the Inquiry-Based Learning Experience: What questions do I still have?

Mining State Standards Template

State Standard	Content and Skills	Lower-Level Expectations (Knowledge and Comprehension)		Higher-Level Expectations (Application, Analysis, Synthesis, and Evaluation)	
		Stated	Implied	Stated	Implied
	Content:				
	Skills:				

Questioning Practices Record

Questioning Practices Record   Sheet 1 of 1

Teacher's Name: _____   Date: _____   Start Time: _____   End Time: _____

Directions: Record each teacher-posed question—including follow up probes and cues—in the first column. Next, classify the question. In the next column, indicate the approximate amount of wait time in seconds. Finally, record who the responder to the question is by using either an "M" for male or "F" for female. Should the teacher call on multiple responders for a question, note a number by each letter to show the order.

Question	Question Level*			Wait Time (seconds)	Responder			
	Recall	Use	Create		Volunteer		Nonvolunteer	
					Males	Females	Males	Females
Directions: Total the information for each column in this row. If multiple sheets were used, write the grand total for each column on the first page and circle those numbers.	Total #	Total #	Total #	Mode	# Males	# Females	# Males	# Females

* Walsh and Sattes' Taxonomy: **Recall** indicates the student is remembering information that was taught; **Use** refers to the student implementing the information taught; and **Create** addresses times when the student must go beyond what was taught to formulate a response.

Rubric Template

Item	Well Done *In addition to meeting the "Good" standard…*	Good	Needs Improvement	Unsatisfactory

Student-Achievement Goal-Setting Form

Teacher's Name: _____

School: _____ Grade: _____ School Year: _____ – _____

I. Setting (Describe the population and special learning circumstances)	
II. Content/Subject/Field Area (The area/topic addressed based on learner achievement, data analysis, or observational data)	
III. Baseline Data (What the current data show)	
IV. Goal Statement (Describe what you want learners/program to accomplish)	

V. Means for Attaining Goal (Activities used to accomplish the goal)

Strategy	Measurable By	Target Completion Date

VI. Mid-Year Review (Describe goal progress and other relevant data)	
VII. End-of-Year Data Results (Accomplishments at the end of year)	

Student Engagement Record

Student Engagement Record

Teacher's Name: _____ Date: _____ Number of Students in the Class: _____ Start Time: _____ End Time: _____

Directions: Draw a heavy line across the table to indicate the number of students in the class during the observation. In five-minute intervals, scan the room counting the number of students who are visibly engaged in the class activity. Mark a line on the bar for the interval at the number of engaged students. Then in the bar, describe what was occurring in the room when the observation was made. Finally, in the last column indicate what the students who were disengaged were doing.

Interval	Class Activity (1–35)	Actions of Visibly Disengaged Students
5		☐ Disrupting Others ☐ Other_____
10		☐ Disrupting Others ☐ Other_____
15		☐ Disrupting Others ☐ Other_____
20		☐ Disrupting Others ☐ Other_____
25		☐ Disrupting Others ☐ Other_____
30		☐ Disrupting Others ☐ Other_____
35		☐ Disrupting Others ☐ Other_____
40		☐ Disrupting Others ☐ Other_____
45		☐ Disrupting Others ☐ Other_____
50		☐ Disrupting Others ☐ Other_____
55		☐ Disrupting Others ☐ Other_____
60		☐ Disrupting Others ☐ Other_____
65		☐ Disrupting Others ☐ Other_____

Column scale: 1 2 3 4 5 6 7 8 9 10 11 12 13 14 15 16 17 18 19 20 21 22 23 24 25 26 27 28 29 30 31 32 33 34 35

Student Progress Monitoring Summary

School: _____

Student Name: _____ Grade: _____

Teacher: _____ Student Monitoring Initiation Date: _____

Student Skill Deficit or Challenge being monitored: _____

Criteria for Success (i.e., at what point will intervention be discontinued?) _____

Student Baseline/Benchmark Data and Progress Scores from Whole-Class Assessment

School-/Districtwide Tool	First Screening Date/Score	Second Screening Date/Score	Third Screening Date/Score	Fourth Screening Date/Score

Interventions Provided to Address Identified Skill Deficit Above:

Intervention Description	Start Date	End Date	Criterion Met?

Individual Student Curriculum-Based Measurement (CBM) Results:

CBM Used	Date/Score	Date/Score	Date/Score	Date/Score	Date/Score	Date/Score

Student Progress Monitoring Completion Date (if applicable): _____

Use the back of this form for narrative progress notes and additional attached sheets for charts and graphs of CBM scores.

Table of Specifications

Content/Subject Matter	Thinking Level Required			
	Knows	Understands	Applies	Total
Total				

Technology Integration Planning

Standard:									

Step 1: Unpack the curriculum for content and cognitive level	Knowledge	Comprehension	Application	Analysis	Synthesis	Evaluation	**Step 2:** Choose an Appropriate Instructional Strategy	**Step 3:** Examine Technology Tools Available	**Step 4:** Decide on the most appropriate technology tool to use with curriculum and instructional strategy
Content:							*Possible Strategies:*		
							Chosen Strategy:		

Tiered Lesson Plan Template

Tiered Lesson Plan Template

Teacher:	Grade Level/Subject:

Topic:

Local, State, or National Standard:

Essential Understanding(s):

Type of Differentiation:	**Portion of Lesson Tiered:**
☐ Academic readiness, based on _____ ☐ Student interest, based on _____ ☐ Learning preference, based on _____	☐ Content ☐ Process ☐ Product

Lesson Description:

Teacher-Provided Materials:

Tiered Element Description:

Tier 1—

Tier 2—

Tier 3—

Assessment:

Part III

Annotated Bibliography and References

Annotated Bibliography Related to Teaching and Learning

This annotated bibliography is provided for readers who would like to learn more about teaching and learning from selected research and professional literature. Some studies and articles in this section were briefly introduced in a particular chapter but were not explained in detail. Others were not mentioned in the book but nonetheless offer additional information on best practices related to a specific topic. The annotations are presented in a standard format for ease in referencing the information.

Matrix

The matrix that follows is intended as a guide to connect the annotations with key aspects or issues related to the overall topic of teaching and learning. The first column contains the authors' last names. The second column provides a link between the annotation and the appropriate chapter. The final column denotes the specific topic addressed in the annotation.

Reference	Chapter	Topic
Australian Journal of Language and Literacy (2005)	2	Literacy differentiation
Bell, Smetana, & Binns (2005)	3	Inquiry instruction
Broekkamp, Van Hout-Wolters, Van der Bergh, & Rijlaarsdam (2004)	4	Assessment/teacher-made tests
Burts, McKinney, Gilmore, & Ford (1985)	3	Concept instruction
Byrum, Jarrell, & Munoz (2002)	2	Lesson study
Chappuis (2005)	4	Helping students understand assessment
Fuchs, Fuchs, & Compton (2004)	4	Reading assessment
Fuchs, Fuchs, Finelli, Courey, Hamlett, Sones, & Hope (2006)	3	Problem-solving instruction
Gioka (2007)	4	Formative feedback / assessment
Helm (2004)	3	Project-based learning
Judson (2006)	2	Technology
Lubienski (2006)	3	Instructional practices, achievement gap
Matsumara, Patthey-Chavez, Valdes, & Garnier (2002)	4	Writing feedback
Notar, Zuelke, Wilson, & Yunker (2004)	4	Accountability/teacher-made tests
Parker, Murname, City, & Moody (2005)	4	Using assessment to improve instruction
Schwartz, Sadler, Sonnert, & Tai (2009)	2	Content coverage: depth versus breadth
Shute (2007)	4	Formative feedback
Speece, Case, & Molloy (2003)	4	Reading disability assessment
VanTassel-Baska (2002)	4	Assessment of gifted learners in language arts
Vaughn, Linan-Thompson, & Hickman (2003)	2	Response to intervention
Wimer, Ridenour, Thomas, & Place (2001)	3	Questioning and gender
Woods & Anderson (2002)	4	Rubrics

Australian Journal of Language and Literacy. (2005). Literacy teaching practice: Differentiation. *Australian Journal of Language and Literacy, 28*(3), 225–231. [Journal article]

Researchers examined the literacy differentiation practices of 11 elementary teachers: four less-effective, five effective, and two more-effective teachers. "Effectiveness" was determined through an analysis of students who had learned (a) more than expected during the school year, (b) about the same, and (c) less than expected. The researchers observed teachers in terms of the following five key aspects of differentiation:

- *Challenge*—Lessons should promote higher-level thinking and should be matched to the students' abilities.

- *Individualization*—Lessons should take into account and be modified for individual student needs.

- *Inclusion*—Lessons should engage all students.

- *Variation*—Lessons should incorporate flexible grouping to respond to individual student needs.

- *Connection*—Lessons should encourage students to "connect" with the concepts being studied by incorporating new literacy concepts into existing schema.

The teachers were videotaped teaching and the videos were coded by frequency for occurrences of the five dimensions listed above. Overall, the researchers found that practices related to differentiation were more frequently used by more-effective teachers and by effective teachers than by less-effective teachers. The differences between more-effective/effective teachers and less-effective teachers are described in the table below.

	More-Effective and Effective Teachers	**Less-Effective Teachers**
Challenge	Used a variety of challenging activities to meet the needs of students	Used questioning throughout lesson, but questions were mainly lower level and focused on one correct answer rather than divergent thinking
Individualization	Focused on individual student needs and provided feedback to students based on their progress	Were aware of individual student needs, but this awareness did not translate into action
Inclusion	Modified instruction based on individual needs so that all students were included in the lesson	Knew individual student needs but failed to act on that knowledge, resulting in student disengagement

Variation	Used a variety of strategies and groupings to meet student needs, including instruction focused on *content* needs and *student* needs	Failed to use flexible grouping to meet individual student needs
Connection	Used student background knowledge, family relationships, and community relationships to help make connections with literature	Failed to incorporate student background knowledge and family and community relationships in a systematic, deliberate way

Adeptly differentiated instruction was the result of conscientious actions on the part of the effective and more effective teachers. The researchers concluded, "Providing a successful differentiated curriculum is a complex and demanding task, through which effective teachers assist children to make connections between the 'known' and the 'new'" (p. 225).

Bell, R. L., Smetana, L., & Binns, I. (2005). Simplifying inquiry instruction: Assessing the inquiry level of classroom activities. *The Science Teacher, 72*(7), 30–33. Retrieved March 8, 2006, from http://find.galegroup.com. [Journal article]

This article discusses the various levels of inquiry so that teachers can assess the cognitive demand that a particular activity will place on students. A teacher scaffolds experiences for students so that students' abilities increase from lower-level thinking skills to higher levels of inquiry. The authors remind readers that inquiry is an active learning process in which students move among four levels of inquiry, depending on their skill and knowledge level. For example, a student may have prior knowledge that enables her to conduct a guided-inquiry investigation, yet the next unit of study may be largely new information, so the student needs a lower level of inquiry investigation to build understanding. The four levels of inquiry are identified in the table below, with the level of complexity of the inquiry increasing from top to bottom.

Inquiry Level	Explanation	Example Using Solutions
Confirmation	This is the most basic level of inquiry in which students are verifying something that is already known.	The amount of a solute affects the density of a solution. Varying saltwater concentrations will be used to demonstrate this principle.
Structured	Students answer a teacher-provided question using a teacher-provided procedure.	Follow the procedure to layer the different colors of saltwater in a test tube in order to determine the relationship between density and the amount of solute in a solution.

Guided	Students design a procedure to answer a teacher-provided question.	During the investigation answer the question: How does the amount of a solute affect the density of the solution? Follow the scientific method and obtain permission from the teacher prior to experimenting.
Open	Students investigate a topic-related question in which they determine the question and procedure.	Design an investigation related to the concepts the class has been studying on solutions. Experiment only after the teacher has approved your procedure.

Students frequently work in groups. Cooperative grouping may cause some challenging responses from teachers and students, such as:

♦ "I don't like group work because I always have to do everything!" (student)

♦ "I hate working in groups because I am ignored." (student)

♦ "How do I make sure everyone in the group participates?" (teacher)

Assigning students roles to assume in a group is one way to address concerns mentioned above, and this works from pre-K through high school, although the roles may vary depending on the content area or activity. The Full Option Science System (FOSS) is just one of many cooperative learning strategies in which mixed-ability students work on an activity together.[1] Every student in the group is responsible for learning the material and participating, and additionally, each person has a role they fulfill for the functioning of the group. Before implementing FOSS, the teacher instructs the students on the various responsibilities of each role. Like other routines, once the teacher invests the time in the explanation and training of students, the classroom runs more smoothly with less time on transitions. Common roles and their respective responsibilities are:

♦ *Reader*—reads all the instructions or related selections

♦ *Writer*—writes the group's ideas, responses, etc.

♦ *Materials manager*—gets items needed for the activity; the only person who can move around the room (e.g., to get water, throw away trash, collect and return supplies, etc.)

♦ *Timer*—ensures the group starts the activity, keeps track of how much time is left, times everything in the experiment, and ensures that the group finishes in the allotted time

♦ *Reporter*—speaks for the group when it is time for all the groups to share their ideas

---

1 Jarrett, D. (1999). *The inclusive classroom: Mathematics and science instruction for students with learning disabilities—It's just good teaching.* Portland, OR: Northwest Regional Educational Laboratory. Retrieved Spring 2003 from http://www.nwrel.org/msec/images/resources/justgood/09.99.pdf

The roles will vary depending on the size of the groups and the requirements of the activity. Oftentimes when FOSS is used, teachers will keep students grouped together for several activities so that students have an opportunity to rotate through all the roles.

♦ Some teachers make name tags that have the role on the front and a bulleted list of responsibilities on the back. The name tag serves as a visual reminder of the student's role for that activity.

♦ Other teachers leave the back of the name tag blank so students can sign their names when they assume a role. In this case, a student cannot repeat a role until everyone has had a chance to do that role.

♦ Still other teachers let students self-monitor and select their own roles.

By providing students with roles, teachers give them the tools to enhance the team's performance. A side benefit is that the number of people moving around the room is greatly reduced because only one person (the materials manager) is allowed to leave the table, which helps with classroom management as well. There is more student ownership of the product because everyone has a vested interest. The type A students who typically try to take over can't do it all because their classmates have specific responsibilities. In addition, reluctant participants are more likely to get involved because the group needs them in order to function.

Broekkamp, H., Van Hout-Wolters, B., Van den Bergh, H., & Rijlaarsdam, G. (2004). Students' expectations about the processing demands of teacher-made tests. *Studies in Educational Evaluation, 30,* 281–304. [Journal article]

A study examined teacher-made tests and the match between teacher expectations of the level of thinking required versus student expectations of the level of thinking required. Twenty-two history teachers who collectively taught 451 students participated in the study. Items on a test were placed into four categories: knowledge, comprehension, analysis/inference, and skill application. Two days prior to a test the researchers asked students to indicate the number of test items in each of the four categories they expected on an upcoming test. Similarly, teachers were asked to indicate the number of test items they expected in each of the four categories on an upcoming test. For each category, students and teachers gave ratings of (a) no questions, (b) few questions, (c) quite a lot of questions, and (d) a great many questions. (The category names are verbatim.) The researchers also asked teachers to classify the actual test items into the four categories. The following table illustrates the findings of this study.

**Relative Ratings of Test Items from Most
Important (1) to Least Important (4)**

	Knowledge	Comprehension	Inference/ Analysis	Skill Application
Teachers' expectations	4	3	1	2
Teachers' actual demands*	2	3	1	2
Students' expectations	4	3	1	2

*Note: This row indicates the relative importance based on actual test content.

The findings indicated that teachers and students had similar expectations in the types of items and the relative emphasis that each would receive. However, when actual test questions were coded, knowledge items were emphasized to a greater degree than both teachers and students expected. The authors recommend that teachers ensure that instruction and test items are aligned in terms of thinking levels required and that expectations are clearly communicated to students.

Burts, D. C., McKinney, C. W., Gilmore, A. C., & Ford, M. J. (1985). The effects of presentation order of examples and nonexamples on first-grade students' acquisition of coordinate concepts. *Journal of Educational Research, 78*(5), 310–314. [Journal article]

A study examined the effects of how concepts are presented to students. The geographic concepts of mountains, hills, tablelands, and plains were introduced. A total of 110 students were assigned to two treatment groups and one control group. The following table shows the type of instruction that was delivered to each treatment group and to the control group.

Group	Instruction
Treatment One: Response-Sensitive Presentation	◆ Students were shown five examples of each of the four landforms. ◆ If students identified the landform correctly, another example of the same landform was shown. ◆ If students identified the landform incorrectly, the teacher gave corrective feedback and then showed an example of the landform that was incorrectly identified. ◆ After the student correctly identified the first concept presented, the teacher moved on.

Treatment Two: Response-Insensitive Presentation	◆ Students were shown five examples of each of the four landforms in a predetermined sequence. ◆ Students were asked to identify landforms, and the teacher provided corrective feedback with explanations. ◆ The landforms were presented in the predetermined order regardless of student response.
Control Group	◆ No instruction on concepts

After instruction, students took a thirty-two–item multiple-choice test in which they were to match landforms to new examples presented. The students in the response-sensitive treatment group scored significantly better on the test than students in the response-insensitive treatment group or in the control group. Students in the response-insensitive treatment group scored significantly better than students in the control group.

The researchers advocate for presenting examples of concepts to respond to students' misunderstandings. For example, if a student identified a mountain as a hill, the teacher showed the student a picture of a hill immediately in order to point out the differences between the two rather than waiting until all pictures of mountains were shown. The key is to respond to errors in logic immediately.

Byrum, J. L., Jarrell, R., & Munoz, M. (2002). *The perceptions of teachers and administrators on the impact of the lesson study initiative.* Louisville, KY: Jefferson County Public Schools. (ERIC Document Reproduction Service No. ED467761) [Report]

One teacher quoted in this study observed, "I don't have to teach in isolation.…Planning and delivering a lesson is a lot more fun and productive when a team of teachers is involved in the process" (p. 13). Lesson study is a collegial activity in which teachers systematically examine their professional practice to enhance the quality of the experiences they provide to their students. Teachers at twenty-five secondary schools in Jefferson County, KY, were invited to participate. They engaged in a process that involved "working collaboratively to set an overarching goal, plan a lesson, design an open response question and scoring guide, teach the lesson, assign the open response question, reflect and make improvements (on the basis of observations of student learning), and then reteach the lesson with the improvements in place" (p.8). Lesson study is a sustained professional development opportunity that provides a forum for teachers to actively use what they are learning with other teachers and their own students. Through the process, high-quality, field-tested lessons were developed.

An action research investigation conducted on the lesson study initiative found that lesson study impacted administrators and teachers. The administrators indicated that they had to be willing to let teachers take the lead as they moved into the more supportive role of ensuring funding for training and release time. The teachers reported several benefits including:

- Collaboration

- Increased awareness of instructional strategies

- Better planning (e.g., planning units with an overarching goal, then designing the assessment, and finally designing the daily lesson)

- Validation of professional practice

- Efficiency of planning together

- Reflecting both individually and together on their instructional practice

Chappuis, S. (2005). Helping students understand assessment. *Educational Leadership, 63(3), 39–43.* [Journal article]

Students, not teachers, control learning. The teacher, in essence, provides a door through which students walk to learn a particular content area or skill. If the door is more attractive, such as an engaging and responsive classroom, then students are more likely to want to invest themselves in learning. The article presents seven strategies to help students understand that assessment can be organized around three questions (all questions are direct quotes from the article):

- *Where am I going?*

  - Strategy 1: Share the learning goals with students.

  - Strategy 2: Show students examples of good and poor work. Then work with the students to identify the components that make each selection strong or weak.

- *Where am I now?*

  - Strategy 3: Offer regular and timely feedback that describes students' actions.

  - Strategy 4: Help students learn how to assess their own work and set meaningful goals based on their self-assessments.

- *How can I close the achievement gap?*

  - Strategy 5: Plan lessons that break learning into manageable components so that students focus on discrete elements before putting it all together.

  - Strategy 6: Encourage students to revise their work, and focus them on a particular aspect during the revision.

  - Strategy 7: Teach students to reflect on their learning.

Fuchs, L. S., Fuchs, D., & Compton, D. L. (2004). Monitoring early reading development in first grade: Word identification fluency versus nonsense word fluency. *Exceptional Children, 71*(1), 7–21. **[Journal article]**

Curriculum-based measurements (CBM) may be used to assess response-to-intervention (RtI). As noted by the researchers of this study, CBM users must be confident "that the measures they use to identify students for expensive, intensive services, in fact, yield the students most at risk for poor reading outcomes" (p. 10). In this study, two curriculum-based measures were compared and used with first grade reading development in an effort to identify appropriate measures for monitoring reading progress in first graders.

One hundred fifty-one first graders from eight public, metropolitan schools, half of which were Title I schools, were identified as at-risk for reading difficulties. With parental consent, these students were incorporated into a peer tutoring intervention and measured for word identification fluency and nonsense word fluency as the two CBM measures. Progress monitoring measures were administered for twenty weeks. The results of this study indicated that using word identification fluency measures provide better assessment of early first grade reading development than nonsense word fluency measures. To that end, these researchers recommended that nonsense word fluency measures be discontinued as a tool for monitoring and assessing reading progress. Finally, additional recommendations included using frequent student monitoring with word identification fluency as a tool in identifying students potentially at risk for reading difficulties.

Fuchs, L. S., Fuchs, D., Finelli, R., Courey, S. J., Hamlett, C. L., Sones, E. M., & Hope, S. K. (2006). Teaching third graders about real-life mathematical problem-solving: A randomized controlled study. *The Elementary School Journal, 106*(4), 293–311. **[Journal article]**

Do real-life problems help third-grade mathematics students perform better at problem solving? In this study, thirty third-grade teachers in an urban school district were randomly assigned to one of three groups:

1. *Control group*—In this group, teachers used a basal text to teach problem solving. Students were taught rules to solve various problems but were not taught how to use the rules to transfer their ability to novel situations. Instruction focused on applying rules and accurate computation.

2. *Schema-broadening instruction*—In this group, students received instruction on how to solve various types of problems. Then they were given problems with slightly different cover stories and taught how to transfer what they had learned to solving novel problems.

3. *Schema-broadening instruction with real-life problems*—Students in this group received similar instruction to the schema-broadening group, but they also were shown videotapes of real-life problems that would require second-

grade mathematics skills. The teacher provided instruction on strategies and how to pick out relevant information for solving real-life problems.

Four hundred fifty-five students in thirty teachers' classes were given a pre- and a posttest with three types of problems (immediate transfer, near transfer, and far transfer) in order to determine whether students could solve novel problems. The researchers' findings were not surprising:

♦ Both groups of students who received schema-broadening instruction performed significantly better on the posttest than students in the control group.

♦ Students who received instruction with real-life problems performed significantly better on the questions that mirrored real life than students who did not receive instruction using real-life problems.

The researchers urged cautious interpretation despite these promising results. While students with instruction in real-life problems performed significantly better in some problem types, they did not perform better in all problem types. As a result, further research into this issue is recommended.

Gioka. O. (2007). Assessment for learning in biology lessons. *Journal of Biological Education, 41*(3), 113–116. [Journal article]

A researcher examined the formative assessment practices of nine secondary-level science teachers in London. Students ranged in age from eleven to eighteen years old. Each teacher was observed teaching science at least ten times, and the lessons were audiotaped. At least one lesson included an investigation in which students obtained data, depicted data in graph form, interpreted data from graphs, drew conclusions, and evaluated the success of the activity. The researcher also collected student investigation reports that had been assessed by the teacher. Their findings reveal varied formative assessment practices, including communication of assessment criteria, oral feedback through questioning, and response dialogue and written feedback on investigative reports. The table below describes what the teachers should be doing according to the research in each area and what they are actually doing.

Area of Investigation	Feedback Research Suggestion of Teacher Actions	What Teachers Did
Communication of criteria to students	♦ Provide students with the criteria for demonstrating achievement according to the learning goal.	♦ Teachers emphasized two types of criteria: what students needed to know and be able to do for the science exam *and* criteria related to the investigative process itself.
Oral feedback through questioning and dialogue	♦ Ask questions that support student learning by challenging their answers and then using subsequent questions that guide students to unpack their thinking. ♦ Indicate quality of response to students. ♦ Encourage students to ask questions themselves.	♦ Teachers dominated the discussion by being the primary generators of questions. ♦ A large proportion of questions focused on recall knowledge. ♦ Three teachers asked higher-order thinking questions that focused on helping students improve their understanding and that linked student responses to the learning goal and to the quality of the response.
Written feedback on investigative reports	♦ Provide comments on assignments related to both the learning goal and the desired attainment of the learning goal.	♦ Teachers commented in the interviews that writing comments is time-consuming and takes great effort on the part of the teacher. ♦ Three teachers gave written, formative feedback that was specific and constructive in nature. ♦ Six teachers gave generic comments such as "Excellent" or "Rewrite."

The researcher concluded that few of these nine teachers used formative assessment. Most teachers did not provide adequate feedback on oral discussions or written assignments. The following recommendations were made based on the results of this study and on literature related to assessment for learning:

♦ Provide science teachers with training to deepen their content knowledge as well as their pedagogical content knowledge so that they are confident in making judgments regarding student work.

♦ Provide science teachers with training on effective practices related to formative assessment, which includes the use of questioning and written feedback to improve student learning.

Helm, J. H. (2004). Projects that power young minds. *Educational Leadership,* *62*(1), 58–62. [Journal article]

The author gave two examples from a kindergarten class studying spiders in which students in both classrooms were engaged, participating, and enjoying the hands-on learning. The distinction between the two examples was the level of involvement of the students and the content. An integrated concepts approach has students making something, counting, identifying, and following directions. A more in-depth approach is to use a project in which interdisciplinary connections are made in an activity that involves students emotionally while challenging them mentally (see chart example). When students are able to initiate learning activities, such as defining questions about spiders, they are motivated to learn academic skills and build their vocabulary. The author wrote, "Project-based learning is an excellent way to make learning meaningful for young children because this is a period of rapid intellectual growth" (p. 59). By providing rich experiences, teachers are supporting young students in making connections and articulating their knowledge.

The following chart shows the phases of a rich project-based learning experience.

	Phase	What Occurs	Example Using Spiders
1	Beginning	The focus is on identifying a topic of interest to students and building on their background knowledge, so the topic can be refined and questions can be developed.	*Defining the concept*—Observe a spider; draw and label a spider; ask questions about spiders.
2	Investigation	This involves collecting resources, helping students or teaching students how to use the resources, recording new questions, and developing ways to recall what was learned.	*Developing the concept*—Read books; identify the similarities and differences between different types of spiders.
3	Culmination	This is the reflection stage in which students think about what was learned and determine how they will share their new knowledge.	*Demonstrating knowledge of the concept*—Write a story about spiders; sketch spider habitats; give a presentation about spiders.

Quality projects lead to higher-level thinking where students are encouraged to predict *how* something might work and seek answers to learn how something *does* work. The topic selected for a project must have potential depth for exploration while also tapping into student interest. "Project topics that inspire curiosity and tap into many subjects increase vocabulary and language competence" (p. 61) because students often produce their best work when they are invested in the topic. Furthermore, when the teacher incorporates the standards and curriculum into the project, students' understanding of the content deepens.

Judson, E. (2006). How teachers integrate technology and their beliefs about learning: Is there a connection? *Journal of Technology and Teacher Education, 14*(3), 581–598. [Journal article]

Are teachers' beliefs about learning and their use of technology in instruction related? The researchers set out to answer this question in their study. Thirty-two teachers completed a survey on instructional beliefs and were also observed using an instrument that measures alignment between constructivist practices and the use of technology in instruction. Although teachers reported that they believed in constructivist practices, they did not necessarily use constructivist practices when using technology in instruction. Teachers said they believed in a student-centered approach to teaching but the observations revealed no relationship between what the teachers reported they believed and what they actually did in the classroom, at least in regards to technology.

The authors of the article discuss the importance of professional development both in constructivist ways of teaching and in the use of technology for instruction. At the same time, they stress that technology integration is not a teaching strategy but rather is a tool that helps students to better understand content. Therefore, integration of technology should be a seamless part of instruction, rather than a sideshow.

Lubienski, S. T. (2006). Examining instruction, achievement, and equity with NAEP mathematics data. *Educational Policy Analysis Archives, 14*(14). Retrieved July 20, 2006, from http://epaa.asu.edu/v14n14/. [Journal article]

The researchers found that the mathematics achievement of 13,511 fourth-grade students who participated in the National Assessment of Academic Progress (NAEP) was positively correlated to the teacher's use of reform-oriented practices. The study also examined differences in instruction for students of various backgrounds. Although instructional practices were similar for black, Hispanic, and white students, black or Hispanic students were more likely to be frequently assessed with multiple-choice tests than were white students.

According to the researchers, "there are large race- and SES-related achievement gaps" that are difficult to explain. Nevertheless, when teachers focused more on problem solving, used more manipulatives, and were aware of the National Council of Teachers of Mathematics (NCTM) standards, their students performed better on the mathematics NAEP. The researchers concluded that more studies are needed to further explore the basis for the remaining achievement gap.

Matsumura, L. C., Patthey-Chavez, G. G., Valdes, R., & Garnier, H. (2002). Teacher feedback, writing assignment quality, and third-grade students' revision in lower- and higher-achieving urban schools. *The Elementary School Journal, 103*(1), 3–25. [Journal article]

Researchers examined the quality of writing assignments, the nature of teacher feedback on writing assignments, and the nature of student revisions from first drafts to the final composition. The study took place in twenty-nine urban third grade classrooms. Thirteen classrooms were sampled from lower-achieving schools and sixteen from higher-achieving schools. The teachers submitted three items to researchers for analysis: (a) a writing assignment and a comprehension assignment analyzed for quality based on a rubric; (b) a one-page description of the assignments, which was also taken into consideration when applying the rubric; and (c) four student work samples, two of medium quality and two of high quality, which were coded for type of feedback provided and then analyzed to determine changes between drafts and final products. Types of feedback included the following:

♦ *Surface level*—feedback focused on mechanics, usage, sentence structure

♦ *Clarification level*—feedback focused on asking for clarification of a word or phrase and its meaning

♦ *Content level*—feedback related to the ideas and actual content contained in the writing sample

Among other areas of interest, the researchers looked at the difference in type of feedback given to students from lower-achieving schools vs. students from higher-achieving schools (see table). Overall, students in lower-achieving schools received more written feedback on both the surface and the content level than did students in higher-achieving schools. However, both groups of students received more feedback related to grammar and mechanics than content.

Comments	Lower-Achieving School Students	Higher-Achieving School Students
Most common type of comments	Surface Level	Surface Level
Mechanics and usage	11.2 average comments	8.1 average comments
Ideas contained in the writing	3.1 average comments	1.5 average comments
None given	21%	55%

The researchers also looked at the relationship between the quality of the writing assignment, the type of feedback received, and the quality of students' work. A significant, positive relationship was found between the quality of the writing assignment and students' work. There was also a significant, positive relationship between type of feedback and quality of student work. Specifically, when students received detailed surface-level comments, the quality of mechanics improved. Likewise, when students received detailed content-level comments, the quality of the content improved. The researchers noted that third grade is a critical year in which students begin to develop in their writing. However, unless feedback and assessment of student work focus on the quality of the content, the overall quality of students' writing will not improve.

Notar, C. E., Zuelke, D. C., Wilson, J. D., & Yunker, B. D. (2004). The table of specifications: Insuring accountability in teacher made tests. *Journal of Instructional Psychology, 31*(2), 115–129. **[Journal article]**

How valid is a student's grade-point average? The answer to this question is simple: It is only as valid as the assessments that make up the student's grades. Accountability of teacher-made tests is necessary to support the use of GPAs for college admission. The authors used the analogy of wedding traditions to explore the validity of teacher-made tests.

♦ *Something old...*

The tests themselves are the "something old" because tests have been a part of American public education for decades. Thus, test questions from the early 1900s are precursors of the multiple-choice, short-answer, and true/false test items so prevalent among tests today.[2]

♦ *Something new...*

The "something new" is the use of an assessment plan to determine the value of each test. The assessment plan takes a broad view of all the assessments administered and how the final grade is determined. The authors suggest listing all assessment activities for the grading period, deciding how many assessments will be used, and finally assigning points to each assessment activity.

♦ *Something borrowed...*

The "something borrowed" is a table of specifications or a blueprint. Test publishing companies use such blueprints to address content validity. The table of specifications or blueprint provides a clear description of the instructional objectives and content/skills that make up a test. The authors maintain that if teacher-made tests are built using a blueprint, the grades, and subsequently the GPAs, will be valid.

♦ *Something blue...*

The something blue is a student whose grade is based on tests that are invalid. In high school the consequential validity of course grades and GPAs is a serious factor. Colleges make decisions on who to admit based on GPA. High school sports teams make decisions on whether a student can play based on GPA. Therefore, students deserve tests that are valid and reliable indications of their learning.

The authors encouraged the use of a table of specifications. They maintained that just as a strong marriage is built on hard work, a teacher-made test that is both valid and reliable requires hard work on the part of the teacher.

---

2 Sheppard, L. (2000). The role of classroom assessment in teaching and learning. *CSE Technical Report, 517.* Retrieved November 15, 2006, from http://www.cse.ucla.edu/Reports/TECH517.pdf

Parker, K. P., Murname, R. J., City, E., & Moody, L. (2005). Teaching educators how to use assessment data to improve instruction. *Phi Delta Kappan, 86*(9), 700–704. [Journal article]

The authors describe a college course in which graduate students, practicing teachers, and practicing administrators engage in data analysis. The graduate-level course was designed for Boston Public Schools educators and for students at the Harvard Graduate School of Education. A key outcome of the class was a change in participants' attitudes towards the use of data in making instructional and program decisions. After participating in the course, the teachers, administrators, and graduate students felt that using data to assess *for* student learning can positively impact school improvement. They also felt more confident in their own ability to use data in this way. The authors concluded, "Our experience indicates that educators can benefit from structured training on how to use student assessment data to improve instruction" (p. 704).

The course was designed around the following key elements:

♦ Providing instruction on data analysis tools.

♦ Using real data.

♦ Collaborating with colleagues to solve real-world problems.

The authors offer advice on how to implement each design element as follows:

Design Element	Recommendations for Implementation
Having a clear process	♦ Recognize the complexity of the data-analysis process. ♦ Focus on each step of the process rather than the process as a whole. ♦ Use data analysis over an extended period of time.
Providing instruction on data analysis tools	♦ Provide explicit, direct instruction on using software for data analysis. ♦ Have participants implement tools that provide data such as tests taken by students or surveys to understand issues related to the use of data from various sources. ♦ Focus on ways to process data and move through the decision-making process.
Using real data	♦ Focus on providing a school context for the data. ♦ Establish expectations and criteria for high-quality work when analyzing data. ♦ Use multiple sources of data in the analysis such as test data, portfolio data, and surveys, but prioritize the types of data to be used. ♦ Discuss issues related to implementing action plans based on data.

Collaborating with colleagues to solve real-world problems	• Form teams of three to four people for optimal size. • Provide time for collaboration, either in class or in a faculty meeting setting. • Establish clear expectations on course requirements and the time commitment involved. • Appoint one team member to serve as a liaison between the data analysis team and the school with which the team is working. • Provide incentives for course completion such as points toward certification.

Schwartz, M. S., Sadler, P. M., Sonnert, G., & Tai, R. H. (2009). Depth versus breadth: How content coverage in high school science courses relates to later success in college science coursework. *Science Education.* **Retrieved 3/11/09 from http://www.interscience.wiley.com/. (***Note:* **released first online.) [Journal article]**

"Students who experience breadth of coverage in high school biology perform in college as if they had experienced half a year *less* preparation than students without breadth of coverage, whereas those who are exposed to in-depth coverage perform as if they had had half a year *more* preparation than the students without depth of coverage" (p.17).

In high school chemistry the difference was one-fourth of a year, and for high school physics it was two-thirds of a year. These findings are from a survey of 8,310 college students in 55 U.S. institutions who were enrolled in a fall introductory science class (i.e., biology, chemistry, or physics). The researchers sought to answer or at least add to the discussion of what is better depth or breadth of coverage in high school science courses.

College students were asked about their high school coursework; for example, introductory physics students were asked about high school physics. They also provided information about their demographics and high school teachers. At the end of the semester, the students' professors provided their grades in the college course. The researchers decided to use the course grade, as introductory classes are the gatekeepers to future study in the subject area and they believed would be more valid than a specially developed test.

The researchers concluded that:

• Depth of coverage (one month spent studying a *big* concept) prepares students better for future study (e.g., higher grades in college courses).

• Breadth of coverage (lots of topics) may result in higher standardized test scores in high school.

• Balancing depth and breadth neither positively nor adversely affected future grades.

The findings were consistent regardless of subject area in the study.

Shute, V. J. (2007). *Focus on formative feedback.* **Princeton, NJ: Educational Testing Service. Retrieved from http://www.ets.org/Media/Research/pdf/ RR-07–11.pdf. [Report]**

Feedback involves providing information to students in order to improve learning. If students do not use the information provided, then the feedback is *not* formative, similar to "If a tree falls in a forest, does anybody hear it fall?" Shute offers some tips on what works and what doesn't work regarding feedback.

♦ *Effective feedback is…*

- directed at the activity rather than the student.

- elaborative on what was done well and what needs improvement.

- enough to direct learning, but not too much so as to overwhelm the student.

- specific to the activity.

- simple but not so simple that it waters down the information or just gives students the correct answer.

- informative about the student's performance on the activity and what the student needs to do in order to accomplish the learning goal.

- objective and not biased by preconceived notions of student performance.

- helpful in moving the student toward learning rather than just focusing on the end result.

- given after the student has attempted the task, not before or during.

♦ *Ineffective feedback is…*

- comparative, with comments focusing on how the student performed in relation to other students.

- accompanied by overall grades.

- demeaning to the student personally.

- overly glowing/false praise.

- detrimental to student learning because it stops learning during a critical time in the activity.

- inevitably revealing the correct answer to the learner.

- given in only one way, without allowing for visual or kinesthetic feedback.

- focused only on analyzing what is not right about the student work and diagnosing only weaknesses.

Timing is also an important consideration related to feedback. Students need to have information at the right time in order to improve their understanding. Shute explains that immediate feedback is appropriate at certain times but at other times delayed feedback is more appropriate. For example, struggling learners may benefit from immediate feedback as they work through a difficult task, but delayed feedback may encourage students to be responsible for their own learning. The chart below provides some guidance on when to use immediate feedback and when to use delayed feedback.

Type of Task	Immediate Feedback	Delayed Feedback
Tasks that are difficult for students	✓	
Tasks that students find relatively easy		✓
Tasks that focus on procedural and conceptual knowledge	✓	
Tasks designed to promote transfer of learning		✓

Speece, D. L., Case, L. P., & Molloy, D. E. (2003). Responsiveness to general education instruction as the first gate to learning disabilities identification. *Learning Disabilities Research & Practice, 18*(3), 147–156. [Journal article]

In this study, researchers conducted a three-year longitudinal study of reading with first and second graders in three suburban schools. Specifically, the researchers sought to investigate the validity of a dual-discrepancy model and response-to-intervention (RtI) as a method of determining reading disabilities in younger children. A dual-discrepancy model used curriculum-based measures (CBMs) in the general education classroom as a tool for determining student *level* and *rate* (i.e., slope), as compared to the student's classroom peers. The student's responsiveness to the intervention was then measured against the student's "dual discrepancy" (p. 147) to determine how the general education instruction should be modified or redesigned to meet the student's identified needs.

After reviewing the data from the study, the researchers concluded that using a "dually-discrepant classification" (p. 149) was a valid indicator identifying younger students with poorer reading performance as compared to their peers. These students were "persistently nonresponsive" (p. 154) to the interventions provided by their general education teachers and had academic and behavioral performance challenges, documenting a need for considerably more intensive interventions (i.e., special education). Additionally, those children classified as being dually discrepant showed improved outcomes and required fewer services outside the classroom when provided with more intensive instruction either through their general education or special education programs.

VanTassel-Baska, J. (2002). Assessment of gifted student learning in language arts. *Journal of Secondary Gifted Education, 13*(2), 67–74. Retrieved January 6, 2006, from http://find.galegroup.com. [Journal article]

Assessment of gifted learners needs to include multiple approaches for assessing student learning, including—but not limited to—rubrics, portfolios, and performance-based assessment. Gifted learners present a unique challenge in many language arts classrooms because they often enter the class reading above grade level, so tests may not adequately measure the high end of students' abilities. Gifted students also need to be challenged at appropriate levels. The use of a rubric provides targeted information to students about each level of performance on each component of the assignment. Descriptions are key to the quality of the feedback provided by the rubric. Rubrics can be used at various points in the learning process such as for preassessment of skills, during the development of an assignment, and as a postassessment to demonstrate growth.

Vaughn, S., Linan-Thompson, S., & Hickman, P. (2003). Response to intervention as a means of identifying students with reading/learning disabilities. *Exceptional Children, 69*(4), 391–409. [Journal article]

In this study, the researchers sought to determine which students of those considered to be at risk for identification with learning disabilities (LD) would respond to reading interventions to the point of no longer being considered at risk for LD. Additionally, the researchers studied student response-to-intervention (RtI) in the general education setting and the appropriateness of using the RtI results as a means for identifying students with LD. Forty-five second graders in Title I schools who were identified as being at-risk for reading challenges were given daily reading instruction using a two-tiered intervention process.

Reading instruction was given to students in ten-week intervals, with students evaluated for progress or potential exit from the intervention program at the end of each ten-week period. The intervention included instruction in fluency, phonemic awareness, instructional level reading, word analysis, and writing. Basal series, trade books, and other published materials were used in the instruction and modifications were made to meet individual needs as indicated by informal assessment.

After the first ten weeks of instruction, ten students met the established exit criteria and no longer received the supplemental instruction. Fourteen students were exited from the program after twenty weeks of instruction. After thirty weeks, another ten students met the exit criteria. At the conclusion of the study, eleven students (i.e., less than 25% of the struggling readers) had not met the exit criteria. Students who met the exit criteria continued to show progress in reading fluency in the general education classroom even without the supplemental interventions. All students profited from the reading interventions, although not equally.

The results of this study supported RtI as a feasible alternative for identifying students with reading disabilities. For those students who do not show progress with supplemental, general education intervention, a special education evaluation may be appropriate. Using the documented results of RtI provides additional criteria for making the often difficult special education decision for students with reading challenges.

Wimer, J. W., Ridenour, C. S., Thomas, K., & Place, A. W. (2001). Higher-order teacher questioning of boys and girls in elementary mathematics classrooms. *The Journal of Educational Research, 95*(2), 84–92. [Journal article]

A research team investigated the degree to which higher-level questions were asked in mathematics classrooms and whether the respondents were boys or girls. Sixteen public and private elementary school classrooms were observed during a mathematics lesson. In general, relatively few higher-order questions were asked of either boys or girls. When a higher-order question was asked, the teacher tended to call on students who had not volunteered a response (twenty-six vs. twelve). Both groups were asked approximately the same number of lower-level questions. The study did find that boys were more likely than girls to be called on in class when they did not volunteer to answer a question.

Woods, M. L., & Anderson, D. (2002). Students designing and applying evaluation rubrics in an aerobics unit. *Physical Educator, 59*(1), 38–57. Retrieved January 6, 2006, from http://find.galegroup.com. [Journal article]

Nineteen ninth-grade physical education students designed an evaluation rubric which they agreed to use for an aerobics unit. Initially, the teacher asked students to design a rubric in small groups. In reviewing the rubrics, the authors noted that there were several commonalities in what student felt should be evaluated. Most students preferred an analytic design in which numbers were assigned to the ratings. The teacher let students vote on a preferred format and solicited additional input. They found that students were reluctant to further develop the rubrics. In the end, the authors synthesized the student-suggested rubrics and presented the product to the students, who were able to recognize elements of their original rubrics. Then students were asked to apply the rubric to their assignment. In analyzing the ratings students gave each other and themselves, the authors found that students concurred on ratings given to peers but tended to rate themselves higher. In general, the authors found that students graded their performance harder than the teacher did.

References

Airasian, P. (1994). *Classroom assessment* (2nd ed., p. 261). New York, NY: McGraw Hill.

Airasian, P. W., & Miranda, H. (2002). The role of assessment in the revised taxonomy. *Theory Into Practice, 41*(4), 249–254.

Amaral, O. M., Garrison, L., & Klentschy, M. (2002). Helping English learners increase achievement through inquiry-based science instruction. *Bilingual Research Journal, 26*(2), 213–239.

Bangert-Downs, R. L., Kulik, C. C., Kulick, J. A., & Morgan, M. (1991). The instructional effects of feedback in test-like events. *Review of Educational Research, 61*(2), 213–54.

Barton-Arwood, S. M., Wehby, J. H., Falk, K. B. (2005). Reading instruction for elementary-aged students with emotional and behavioral disorders: Academic and Behavioral Outcomes. *Exceptional Children, 72*(1), 7–27.

Batsche, G., Elliott, J., Graden, J. L., Grimes, J., Kovaleski, J. F., Prasse, D., Reschly, D. J., Schrag, J., & Tilly III, W. D. (2006). *Response to intervention: Policy considerations and implementation.* Alexandria, VA: National Association of State Directors of Special Education.

Black, P., Harrison, C., Lee, C., Marshall, B., & Wiliam, D. (2003). *Assessment for learning: Putting it into practice.* Philadelphia, PA: Open University Press.

Bloom, B.S. (1984). The search for methods of group instruction as effective one-to-one tutoring. *Educational Leadership, 41*(8), 4–17.

Bloom, B., Englehart, M., Furst, E., Hill, W., & Karthwohl, D. (1956). *Taxonomy of educational objectives: The classification of educational goals. Handbook I: Cognitive domain.* New York, NY: Longmans Green.

Bohn, C. M., Roehrig, A. D., & Pressley, M. (2004). The first days of school in the classrooms of two more effective and four less effective primary grades teachers. *The Elementary School Journal, 104*(4), 269–287. p. 284.

Borko, H. & Livingston, C. (1989). Cognition and improvisation: Differences in mathematics instruction by expert and novice teachers. *American Educational Research Journal, 26*(4), 473–498

Brewster, C., & Fager, J. (2000). *Increasing student engagement and motivation: From time-on-task to homework.* Northwest Regional Educational Laboratory. Retrieved January 5, 2009 from http://www.nwrel.org/request/oct00/textonly.html

Broekkamp, H., Van Hout-Wolters, B., Van den Bergh, H., & Rijlaarsdam, G. (2004). Students' expectations about the processing demands of teacher-made tests. *Studies in Educational Evaluation, 30,* 281–304.

Brown, D. F. (2002). *Becoming a successful urban teacher* (p. 185). Portsmouth, NH: Heinemann.

Brualdi, A. C. (1998). Classroom questions. *ERIC/AE Digest.* Washington, DC: Eric Clearinghouse on Assessment and Evaluation. (ED422407)

Carey, K. (2004). The real value of teachers: Using new information about teacher effectiveness to close the achievement gap. *The Education Trust, 8*(1), 5.

Carolan, J., & Guinn, A. (2007). Differentiation: Lessons from master teachers. *Educational Leadership, 64*(6), 44–46.

Cawelti, G. (2004). *Handbook of research on improving student achievement.* Arlington, VA: Educational Research Service.

The Center for Comprehensive School Reform and Improvement. (2007). *A teacher's guide to differentiating instruction.* Washington, DC: Author.

Clark, D.C. (1971). Teaching concepts in the classroom: A set of teaching prescriptions derived from experimental research. *Journal of Educational Psychology, 62*(2), 253–278.

Committee on Increasing High School Students' Engagement and Motivation to Learn. (2004). *Engaging schools: Fostering high school students' motivation to learn.* Washington, DC: National Academies Press.

Corbett, D, & Wilson, B. (2004). What urban students say about good teaching. *Educational Leadership, 60*(1), 18–22.

Cotton, K. (2000). *Research you can use to improve results.* Portland, OR: Northwest Regional Educational Laboratory.

Cotton, K. (2001). Classroom questioning. *School Improvement Research Series, #5.* Retrieved on January 5, 2009 from www.nwrel.org.scpd/sirs/3/cu5.html

Covino, E. A. & Iwanicki, E. F. (1996). Experienced teachers: Their constructs of effective teaching. *Journal of Personnel Evaluation in Education, 10,* 325–363.

Cradler, J., McNabb, M., Freeman, M., Burchett, R. (2002). How does technology influence student learning? *Learning and Leading with Technology, 29*(8), 46–50.

Csikszenthmihalyi, M., Rathunde, K., & Whalen, S. (1993). *Talented teenagers: The roots of success and failure.* New York, NY: Cambridge University Press.

Darling-Hammond, L. (2000). Teacher quality and student achievement: A review of state policy evidence. *Educational Policy Analysis Archive, 8*(1). Retrieved March 21, 2000, from http://epaa.asu.edu/epaa/v8n1

Darling-Hammond, L., Berry, B., & Thoreson, A. (2001). Does teacher certification matter? Evaluating the evidence. *Educational Policy Analysis, 22*(1), 52–57.

Darling-Hammond, L. (2008). *Powerful learning.* San Francisco, CA: Jossey-Bass.

Duff, V. (n.d.). *Effective lesson planning.* Retrieved June 3, 2005 from www.state.nj.us/education/njpep.org/pd/novice_teacher_resources/effectivelessonplanning.ppt#12

Dunkin, M. J. (1978). Student characteristics, classroom processes, and student achievement. *Journal of Educational Psychology, 70,* 998–1009.

Dunkin, M. J. & Doenau, S. J. (1980). A replication study of unique and joint contributions to variance in student achievement. *Journal of Educational Psychology, 72*(3), 394–403.

Ediger, M. (2004). Psychology of lesson plans and unit development. *Reading Improvement, 41*(4), 197–207.

Education Week. (2008). Standards, assessment, and accountability. *Quality Counts 2008.* Retrieved May 1, 2008, from http://www.edweek.org/media/ew/qc/2008/18sos.h27.saa.pdf.

Educational Research Service. (2001). *Effective teaching: How do we know it when we see it?* The Informed Educator Series. Alexandria, VA: Author.

Emmer, E. T., Evertson, C. M., & Anderson, L. M. (1980). Effective classroom management at the beginning of the school year. *The Elementary School Journal, 80*(5), 219–231.

Felter, M. (1999). High school staff characteristics and mathematics test results. *Educational Policy Analysis Archives, 7*(9). Retrieved December 5, 2000, from http://epaa.asu.edu/epaa/v7n9

Florida Department of Education. (2007). *2007 Read to learn.* Tallahassee, FL: Author. Retrieved January 2, 2009 from http://fcat.fldoe.org/mediapacket/2007/pdf/pressPacketGR3_page16.pdf

Ford, M.J., & McKinney, C.W. (1986). The effects of recycling and response sensitivity on the acquisition of social studies concepts. *Theory and Research in Social Education, 14*(1), 21–33

Fuchs, L. S., Deno, S., & Mirkin, P. (1984). Effects of curriculum-based measurement and evaluation on pedagogy, student achievement, and student awareness of learning. *American Educational Research Journal, 21,* 449–460.

Fuchs, L. S., Fuchs, D., & Compton, D. L. (2004). Monitoring early reading development in first grade: Word identification fluency versus nonsense word fluency. *Exceptional Children, 71*(1), 7–21.

Gardner, H. (1993). *Multiple intelligences: The theory into practice.* New York, NY: Basic Books.

Gamoran, A., Porter, A. C., Smithson, J., & White, P. A. (1997). Upgrading high school mathematics instruction: Improving learning opportunities for low-achieving, low-income youth. *Educational Evaluation and Policy Analysis, 19,* 325–338.

Gareis, C. R., & Grant, L. W. (2008). *Teacher-made assessments: How to connect curriculum, instruction, and student learning.* Larchmont, NY: Eye On Education.

Goldhaber, D. D. & Brewer, D. J. (2000). Does teacher certification matter? High school teacher certification status and student achievement. *Educational Evaluation and Policy Analysis, 22*(2), 129–145.

Good, T. L., & Brophy, J. E. (1997). *Looking in classrooms* (7th ed.). New York, NY: Addison-Wesley.

Gronlund, N. E. (2006). *Assessment of student achievement* (8th ed.). Boston, MA: Pearson.

Guskey, T. R. (2003). How classroom assessments improve learning. *Educational Leadership, 60*(5), 6–11.

Guthrie, J. T., Van Meter, P., Hancok, G. R., Alao, S., Anderson, E., & McCann, A. (1998). Does concept-oriented reading instruction increase strategy use and conceptual learning from text? *Journal of Educational Psychology, 90*(2), 261–278.

Hargreaves, E. (2005). Assessment for learning? Thinking outside the (black) box. *Cambridge Journal of Education, 35*(2), 213–224.

Harris, J. (2008). TPCK in inservice education: Assisting experienced teachers' "planned improvisations." In American Association of colleges for Teacher Education (Ed.), *Handbook of technological pedagogical content knowledge for teaching and teacher educators.* New York, NY: Routledge.

Hattie, J., & Timperley, H. (2007). The power of feedback. *Review of Educational Research, 77*(1), 81–112.

Hawk, P. P., Coble, C. R., & Swanson, M. (1985). Certification: Does it matter? *Journal of Teacher Education, 36*(3), 13–15.

Haycock, K. (2000). No more settling for less. *Thinking K-16, 4*(1), 3–12.

Hiebert, J., Stigler, J. W., Jacobs, J. K., Givvin, K. B., Garnier, H., Smith, M., Hollingsworth, H., Manaster, A., Wearne, D., & Gallimore, R. (2005). Mathematics teaching in the United States today (and tomorrow): Results from the TIMSS 1999 video study. *Educational Evaluation and Policy Analysis, 27*(2), 111–132.

Hogan, T. P. (2007). *Educational assessment: A practical introduction.* Hoboken, NJ: John Wiley & Sons.

Hunnicut, R. C., & Larkins, A.G. (1985). An experimental comparison of three methods of using examples and nonexamples to teach social studies concepts. *Journal of Instructional Psychology, 12*(3), 144–151.

Husen, T. (1967). *International study of achievement in mathematics.* New York, NY: John Wiley & Sons.

INTASC. (1992). *Model standards for beginning teacher licensing, assessment, and development: A resource for state dialogue.* Washington, DC: Author.

Jay, J. K. (2002). Points on a continuum: An expert/novice study of pedagogical reasoning. *The Professional Educator, 24*(2), 63–74.

Johnson, B. L. (1997). An organizational analysis of multiple perspectives of effective teaching: Implications for teacher evaluation. *Journal of Personnel Evaluation in Education, 11,* 69–87.

Joyce, B., & Weil, M. (2004). *Models of teaching.* Boston, MA: Allyn and Bacon.

Klem, A. M., & Connell, J. P. (2004). Relationships matter: Linking teacher support to student engagement and achievement. *Journal of School Health, 74*(7), 262–273.

Krathwohl, D. R. (2002). A revision of Bloom's taxonomy: An overview. *Theory Into Practice, 41*(4), 212–218.

Leithwood, K., Louis, K. S., Anderson, S., & Wahlstrom, K. (2004). *How leadership influences student learning.* Learning From Research Project.

Martin, R., Sexton, C., & Gerlovich, J. (2001). *Teaching science for all children* (3rd ed.). Boston, MA: Allyn and Bacon.

Marx, R. W., Blumenfeld, P. C., Krajcik, J. S., Fishman, B., Soloway, E., Geier, R., & Tali Tal, R. (2004). Inquiry-based science in the middle grades: Assessment of learning in urban systemic reform. *Journal of Research in Science Teaching, 41*(10), 1063–1080.

Marzano, R. (2006). *Classroom assessment and grading that works.* Alexandria, VA: Association for Supervision and Curriculum Development.

Marzano, R. J., Pickering, D., McTighe, J. (1993). *Assessing student outcomes: Performance assessment using the dimensions of learning model.* Alexandria, VA: Association for Supervision and Curriculum Development.

Marzano, R. J., Pickering, D. J., & Pollock, J. E. (2001). *Classroom instruction that works: Research-based strategies for increasing student achievement.* Alexandria, VA: Association for Supervision and Curriculum Development.

Mason, D. A., Schroeter, D. D., Combs, R. K., & Washington, K. (1992). Assigning average-achieving eighth graders to advanced mathematics classes in an urban junior high. *The Elementary School Journal, 92*(5), 587–599.

Matsumura, L. C., Patthey-Chavez, G. G., Valdes, R., & Garnier, H. (2002). Teacher feedback, writing assignment quality, and third-grade students' revision in lower- and higher-achieving urban schools. *The Elementary School Journal, 103*(1), 3–25.

McBer, H. (2000). *Research into teacher effectiveness: A model of teacher effectiveness* (research report #216). London, UK: Department for Education and Employment.

McCaffrey, D. F., Hamilton, L. S., Stecher, B., Klein, S. P., Bugliari, D., & Robyn, A. (2001). Interactions among instructional practices, curriculum, and student achievement: The case of standards-based high school mathematics. *Journal for Research in Mathematics Education, 32*(5), 493–517.

McEachron, G. A. (2001). *Self in the world: Elementary and middle school social studies.* Boston, MA: McGraw-Hill.

Mendro, R. L. (1998). Student achievement and school and teacher accountability. *Journal of Personnel Evaluation in Education, 12,* 257–267.

Merrill, C., & Comerford, M. (2004). Technology and mathematics standards: An integrated approach—A more open-ended and broader definition or meaning of mathematics is the study of patterns. *The Technology Teacher, 64*(2), 10.

Merrill, M.D., & Tennyson, R.D. (1977). *Teaching concepts: An instructional design guide.* Englewood Cliffs, NJ: Educational Technology Publications.

Miller, J. E., McKenna, M. C., & McKenna, B. A. (1998). A comparison of alternatively and traditionally prepared teachers. *Journal of Teacher Education, 49*(3), 165–176.

Mishra, P., & Koehler, M. J. (2006). Technological pedagogical content knowledge: A framework for teacher knowledge. *Teachers College Record, 108*(6), 1017–1054.

Molnar, A., Smith, P., Zahorik, J., Palmer, A., Halbach, A., & Ehrle, K. (1999). Evaluating the SAGE program: A pilot program in targeted pupil-teacher reduction in Wisconsin. *Educational Evaluation and Policy Analysis, 21*(2), 165–178.

National Association of Secondary School Principals. (1997). Students say: What makes a good teacher? *NASSP Bulletin, 3,* 15–17.

National Board for Professional Teaching Standards. (2002). *What teachers should know and be able to do.* Retrieved January 2, 2009 from http://www.nbpts.org/UserFiles/File/what_teachers.pdf.

National Council for Accreditation of Teacher Education. (2008). *Professional standards for the accreditation of schools, colleges, and departments of education.* Retrieved January 2, 2009 from http://www.ncate.org/documents/standards/NCATE%20Standards%202008.pdf.

National Research Council. (1999). *How people learn: Bridging research and practice.* Washington, DC: National Academy Press.

Noonan, B. & Duncan, C. R. (2005). Peer and self-assessment in high schools. *Practical Assessment, Research, and Evaluation, 10*(17), 1–8.

Notar, C. E., Zuelke, D. C., Wilson, J. D., & Yunker, B. D. (2004). The table of specifications: Insuring accountability in teacher made tests. *Journal of Educational Psychology, 31*(2), 115–129.

Nye, B., Konstantopoulos, S., & Hedges, L. V. (2004). How large are teacher effects? *Educational Evaluation and Policy Analysis, 26,* 237–257.

Ornstein, A. C. & Hunkins, F. P. (2004). *Curriculum: Foundations, principles, and issues.* Boston, MA: Allyn & Bacon.

Osmond, S. P., & Jansson, L. C. (1987). Sequencing examples and nonexamples to facilitate concept attainment. *Journal for Research in Mathematics Education, 18*(2), 112–125.

Partnership for 21st Century Skills. (2007). *21st Century skills assessment.* Tucson, AZ: Author. Retrieved January 2, 2009 from http://www.21stcenturyskills.org/documents/21st_century_skills_assessment.pdf.

Peart, N. A., & Campbell, F. A. (1999). At-risk students' perceptions of teacher effectiveness. *Journal for a Just and Caring Education, 5*(3), 269–284.

Pierce, R. L., & Adams, C. M. (2004). Tiered lessons: One way to differentiate mathematics instruction. *Gifted Child Today, 27*(2), 58–66.

Ralph, E. G., Kesten, C., Lang, H., & Smith, D. (1998). Hiring new teachers: What do school districts look for? *Journal of Teacher Education, 49*(1), 47–56.

Rathunde, K., & Csikszetnmihalyi, M. (2005). Middle school students' motivation and quality of experience: A comparison of Montessori and traditional school environments. *American Journal of Education, 111*(3), 341–371.

Robertson, C., & Acklam, R. (2000). *Action plan for teachers: A guide for teaching English.* London, UK: BBC World Service. Retrieved June 3, 2005 from http://www.teachingenglish.org.uk/sites/teachingeng/files/Action_Plan.pdf

Rowan, B., Harrison, D. M., & Hayes, A. (2004). Using instructional logs to study mathematics curriculum and teaching in the early grades. *The Elementary School Journal, 105*(1), 103–128.

Rowe, M. B. (1972). *Wait time and rewards as instructional variables, their influence in language, logic, and fate control.* Chicago, IL: National Association for Research in Science Teaching. (ERIC ED 061103)

Sadler, P. M., & Good, E. (2006). The impact of self- and peer-grading on student learning. *Educational Assessment, 11*(1), 1–31.

Schachter, J. (1999). *The impact of education technology on student achievement: What the most current research has to say.* Santa Monica, CA: Milken Exchange on Educational Technology.

Schafer, W., Swanson, G., Gene, N., Newberry, G. (2001). Effects of teacher knowledge of rubrics on student achievement in four content areas. *Applied Measurement in Education, 14*(2), 151–170.

Schwartz, M. S., Sadler, P. M., Sonnert, G., & Tai, R. H. (2009). Depth versus breadth: How content coverage in high school science courses relates to later success in college science coursework. *Science Education*. Retrieved March 11, 2009 from http://www.interscience.wiley.com/

Shellard, E., & Protheroe, N. (2000). *Effective teaching: How do we know it when we see it?* (The Informed Educator Series). Arlington, VA: Educational Research Service.

Shernoff, D. J., Csikszentmihalyi, M., Schneider, B., & Shernoff, E. S. (2003). Student engagement in high school classrooms from the perspective of flow theory. *School Psychology Quarterly, 18*(2), 158–176.

Singham, M. (2001). The achievement gap. *Phi Delta Kappan, 84*, 586.

Sit, K. H. (2001). Facilitating the shift from the "tell me" to involve me" in GER. *CDTLink, 5*(3), 4–6.

Snipes, J., Doolittle, F., Herlihy, C. (2002). *Foundations for success: Case studies of how urban school systems improve student achievement.* New York, NY: MDRC.

Speece, D. L., Case, L. P., & Molloy, D. E. (2003). Responsiveness to general education instruction as the first gate to learning disabilities identification. *Learning Disabilities Research & Practice, 18*(3), 147–156.

Stahl, R. J. (1994). *Using "think-time" and "wait-time" skillfully in the classroom* (Eric Digest). Bloomington, IN: ERIC Clearinghouse for Social Studies/Social Science Education. (ED 370885).

Stecker, P. M., & Lembke, E. S. (2005, July 8). *Advanced applications of CBM in reading: Instructional decision-making strategies manual.* National Center on Progress Monitoring. Retrieved December 20, 2006 from http://www.studentprogress.org/library/Training/CBMmath/AdvancedReading/AdvRdgManual-FORMATTEDSept29.pdf

Stiggins, R.J. (1997). *Student-centered classroom assessment* (2nd ed). Upper Saddle River, NJ: Merrill.

Stiggins, R. J. (2002). Assessment crisis: The absence of assessment FOR learning. *Phi Delta Kappan, 83*(10) [electronic version]. Retrieved November 11, 2008 from http://80-web2.infotrac.galegroup.com

Stronge, J. H. (2002). *Qualities of effective teachers.* Alexandria, VA: Association for Supervision and Curriculum Development.

Stronge, J. H. (2007). *Qualities of effective teachers* (2nd ed.). Alexandria, VA: Association for Supervision and Curriculum Development.

Stronge, J. H., Gareis, C. R., & Little, C. A. (2006). *Teacher pay and teacher quality: Attracting, developing, & retaining the best teachers.* Thousand Oaks, CA: Corwin Press.

Stronge, J. H., & Grant, L. W. (2009). *Student achievement goal setting: Using data to improve teaching and learning.* Larchmont, NY: Eye On Education.

Stronge, J. H., Tucker, P. D., & Ward, T. J. (2003, April). *Teacher effectiveness and student learning: What do good teachers do?* Chicago, IL: American Educational Research Association Annual Meeting.

Stronge, J. H., Ward, T. J., & Grant, L. W. (2009). *Teacher quality and student learning: What do good teachers do?* Manuscript submitted for publication.

Stronge, J. H., Ward, T. J., Tucker, P. D., & Hindman, J. L. (2008). What is the relationship between teacher quality and student achievement? An exploratory study. *Journal of Personnel Evaluation in Education, 20*(3–4), 165–184.

Taylor, B. M., Pearson, P. D., Peterson, D. S., & Rodriquez, M. C. (2003). Reading growth in high-poverty classrooms: The influence of teacher practices that encourage cognitive engagement in literary learning. *The Elementary School Journal, 104*(1), 121–135.

Tomlinson, C. A. (1999). *The differentiated classroom: Responding to the needs of all learners.* Alexandria, VA: Association for Supervision and Curriculum Development.

Tomlinson, C. A. (2000). *Differentiation of instruction in the elementary grades.* (Report No. EDO-PS-00–7). Champaign, IL: Clearinghouse on Elementary and Early Childhood Education.

Tomlinson, C. A., & Eidson, C. C. (2003). *Differentiation in practice: A resource guide for differentiating curriculum.* Alexandria, VA: Association for Supervision and Curriculum Development.

Tucker, P. D. & Stronge, J. H. (2005). *Linking teacher evaluation and student learning.* Alexandria, VA: Association for Supervision and Curriculum Development.

U.S. Department of Education. (1998). *Promising practices: New ways to improve teacher quality.* Retrieved October 15, 2009 from http://www.ed.gov/pubs/PromPracticeI

Van der Veer, R. (1998). From concept attainment to knowledge formation. *Mind, Culture and Activity, 5*(2), 89–94.

VanTassel-Baska, J. (2005). Gifted programs and services: What are the nonnegotiables? *Theory into Practice, 44*(2), 90–97.

Vaughn, S., & Fuchs, L. S. (2003). Redefining learning disabilities as inadequate response to instruction: The promise and potential pitfalls. *Learning Disabilities Research & Practice, 18*(3), 137–146.

Vaughn, S., Linan-Thompson, S., & Hickman, P. (2003). Response to intervention as a means of identifying students with reading/learning disabilities. *Exceptional Children, 69*(4), 391–409.

Virginia Department of Education. (2003). *English standards of learning curriculum framework.* Richmond, VA: Author. Retrieved May 1, 2009 from http://www.doe.virginia.gov

Virginia Department of Education. (2006). *Music standards of learning for Virginia Public Schools.* Richmond, VA: Author.

Virginia Department of Education. (2006). *A summary of graduation requirements for Virginia Public Schools.* Richmond, VA: Author. Retrieved January 2, 2009 from http://www.doe.virginia.gov/2plus4in2004/index.shtml

Virginia Department of Education. (2008). *United States history standards.* Richmond, VA: Author. Retrieved January 2, 2009 from http://www.doe.virginia.gov

Walberg, H. J. (1984). Improving the productivity of America's schools. *Educational Leadership, 41*(8), 19–27.

Walsh, J. A., & Sattes, B. D. (2005). *Quality questioning: Research-based practice to engage every learner* (p. 23). Thousand Oaks, CA: Corwin Press.

Wang, J. (1998). Opportunity to learn: The impacts and policy implications. *Educational Evaluation and Policy Analysis, 20*(3), 137–156.

Wenglinsky, H. (1998). *Does it compute? The relationship between educational technology and student achievement in mathematics.* Princeton, NJ: Educational Testing Service.

Wenglinsky, H. (2000). *How teaching matters: Bringing the classroom back into discussions of teacher quality.* Princeton, NJ: Educational Testing Service.

Wenglinsky, H. (2002). How schools matter: The link between teacher classroom practices and student academic performance. *Education Policy Analysis Archives, 10*(12). Retrieved October 15, 2009, from http://epaa.asu.edu/epaa/v10n12/

Wenglinsky, H. (2004). The link between instructional practice and the racial gap in middle schools. *Research in Middle Level Education Online, 28*(1), Retrieved January 2, 2009 from http://www.nmsa.org/Publications/RMLEOnline/tabid/101?Default.aspx

Wharton-McDonald, R., Pressley, M., & Hampston, J. M. (1998). Literacy instruction in nine first-grade classrooms: Teacher characteristics and student achievement. *The Elementary School Journal, 99*(2), 101–128.

Wilen, W. (2001). Exploring myths about teacher questioning in the social studies classroom. *The Social Studies, 92*(1), 26–32.

Wisconsin Department of Public Instruction. (July 6, 2006). *Response to intervention.* Retrieved October 15, 2009, from http://dpi.wi.gov/rti/index.html

Wright, S. P., Horn, S. P., & Sanders, W. L. (1997). Teacher and classroom context effects on student achievement: Implications for teacher evaluation. *Journal of Personnel Evaluation in Education, 11,* 57–67.

Yesseldyke, J., & Bolt, D. M. (2007). Effect of technology-enhanced continuous progress monitoring on math achievement. *School Psychology Review, 36*(3), 453–467.

Yin, C. C., & Kwok, T. T. (1999). Multimodels of teacher effectiveness: Implications for research. *The Journal of Educational Research, 92* (3), 141–158.